BE YOU BRAND

Your **story**, Your **business**, Your **way**!

ATI GRINSPUN

ALONG WITH 6 OTHER INSPIRING WOMEN AUTHORS

FOREWORD

Be You Brand: Your Story, Your Business, Your Way

Being your own brand is so much more than just running your business.

It all starts with wanting more freedom, time, not having to answer to anyone, and the many reasons women start businesses.

But it is when we dig deep within ourselves that we realize we chose that business for a reason beyond money, that we have a message to bring to the world.

That message, that often we think does not matter, and the moment we see it does, it lights up a fire so big it cannot be put away. That is being your own brand—Using your story to leave your mark in the world.

This book is THAT. The igniting spark for our readers to discover their flame.

To realize within themselves that if one person, one life is changed by your story, your ripple effect will live forever.

To the dreamers, to the doers, and to the ones who never stop looking for growth within themselves: Go leave your mark in the world.

Each of the chapters in this book, their stories, will validate you, help you, teach you, and inspire you to Be YOU Brand.

Love, Light & Cheers,
Ati

INTRODUCTION

Welcome to *Be You Brand: Your Story, Your Business, Your Way!* – a guide that celebrates not just participating in the business world but revolutionizing it. If you've ever felt the call to create something truly authentic, something that reflects your essence and your experiences, this book is for you.

In these pages, you'll meet remarkable women who are not only navigating their entrepreneurial journeys but are also rewriting the playbook. They're living proof that success is not about fitting into a mold but about breaking it to forge a path uniquely their own. Through their stories, you'll discover how they've harnessed their personal narratives to build brands that stand out, inspire, and make a lasting impact.

Each chapter is a window into a different world of possibilities, revealing the powerful connection between personal authenticity and business success. You'll learn about the art of brand-building, the resilience required to overcome setbacks, and the crucial steps to becoming the CEO of your own life. This book is more than a guide; it's a call to action for every woman who dreams of more than just financial freedom – it's for those who wish to be seen, to inspire, and to effect meaningful change.

So, if you're ready to embrace your true self and redefine what it means to be a leader in your field, dive into *Be You Brand*. Let these stories ignite your passion and equip you with the tools to transform your vision into reality. Welcome to a journey of empowerment, authenticity, and success. Welcome to *Be You Brand*.

TABLE OF CONTENTS

Ati Grinspun

ATI.G.BRANDING LLC
Personal Branding and Business Coach

https://www.linkedin.com/in/ati-grinspun-38b144165/
www.facebook.com/groups/personalbrandingforwomenpreneurs
https://www.instagram.com/ati.g.branding/
https://atigrinspun.com/

Ati is an acclaimed Personal Branding and Business Coach, Speaker, and podcaster, dedicated to empowering dynamic female entrepreneurs. With her infectious energy, she simplifies the complexities of online and offline visibility, making it both manageable and fun. As the visionary founder of "Be You Brand movement," she's on a mission to catapult women to new heights in their fields, believing that their success sparks global positive change.

Pay It Forward. Change the World.

By Ati Grinspun

BE THE CHANGE YOU WANT TO SEE IN THE WORLD.
Mahatma Gandhi

It was a cold Monday morning in March 2019, and I had recently quit my 6-figure, comfy, fun, low-responsibility, I-could-not-do-it-anymore, I-was-so-over-it job.

I had been building my photography business for almost a decade on the side, and I had taken on another small business venture (network marketing) that had lit a FIRE under my butt. It was looking awesome back in December 2018 when I quit…

Until shit. got. real.

When it was time to put myself out there (online, networking events, selling my idea, talking to people, creating content, AND OWNING MY GENIUS AND MY VISION), I was blindsided.

I started doubting every step.

I started having the PHYSICAL feeling like I was spiraling down.

I would find myself at my desk daily, TERRIFIED.

I was looking at the computer screen, and I HAD NO IDEA WHAT TO SAY, WHAT TO POST, or even what I was doing…

Now, for context, this was not my first business. I had owned a VERY successful bartending school back in Argentina, and I had been investing in real estate for years.

But this time, I was the face of this brand. I was the face of this business.

I was selling ME.

So the fear and the limiting beliefs (I didn't even know about those back then!) started arising everywhere.

Does it sound familiar? Maybe like me, you had a job that made you a lot of money and you were so good at it, but you lost the passion for it, or you just wanted more.

Maybe you were a rockstar in your corporate job. You climbed the corporate ladder to realize that was not what you wanted.

Me? I was a world-champion flair bartender. You probably never heard of it; so here it is in short:

I was one of those bartenders who spit fire and flipped bottles. I got to travel all over the world competing and working at a renowned Flair Bar in Las Vegas!

But the moment I stopped competing, I realized I was done with that life. The job itself no longer gave me the passion I was looking for. I WANTED MORE.

I WAS CRAVING CONNECTION, COMMUNITY, AND PURPOSE.

I mean, I could flip glass bottles and spit fire… but the moment I had to talk about my business, sell, share my story, and be the face of it all… PARALYSIS hit me.

The truth is, it's impossible to see the label of the jar you're in. Seeing our own greatness is harder than it sounds.

It's impossible to even know what other people ALREADY see in you.

Because for you, THIS IS YOUR NORMAL.

Back to that cold Monday morning in 2019… I had such a strong MIND GAME.

Not in a positive way. Quite the opposite. I had a voice inside my head, saying:

- Who cares about what YOU have to say?
- Everyone is doing something similar.
- You don't have anything "special."
- Who is going to listen to a "bartender"?

Oh girl, I was SO wrong, AND SO ARE YOU when you think those things, or let ANY kind of mind game stop you from what you KNOW is for you.

This is a fact. But it took me a long road of self-discovery and inner work to BELIEVE that beyond the clichés. If I had only allowed myself to believe it before… I would have saved a lot of tears and time and made money a lot faster.

That, right there, is the reason for the existence of this book.

Helping more women realize, internalize, and truly believe that every single one of us has a different path, a different combination of lived experiences, that shape our points of view, beliefs, cultures, ways of dealing with challenges, and things that spark ideas. And THAT IS ENOUGH.

So even if two people do the same thing … NOT TWO PEOPLE CAN DO IT THE SAME WAY.

This means your way is unique if you allow yourself to BE YOU. Innately, you do not need to fake anything.

Nobody can be you. AND THAT IS ENOUGH. AND THAT IS ALL YOU NEED TO GET STARTED.

The Be You Brand Truth

It's so clear now, 6 years later, writing this chapter of a book I lead for other women and having done the work to build a profitable and authentic personal brand.

So let me set the bar straight here...

Even if you have "the pesky voices" and you are self-critical and a perfectionist; even if the imposter syndrome is eating you alive... no matter if you are working on a new idea or have been in business for a while, LEAN IN...

Because I'm about to show you WHY your biggest job is to GET CLEAR ON WHO YOU ARE AND WHAT YOU BRING TO THE TABLE... YOUR TRUTH, SO YOU, YES, YOU, MY FRIEND, can change the world (and make a shit load of money in the process).

I know you probably had a tiny voice in your head, dismissing what you just read. Like you almost didn't believe it.

So, let me stop you right here and show you how we do it in my world.

Inside the Be You Brand Academy (my personal brand-focused business program) we often talk about THE BE YOU BRAND TRUTH - your CORE TRUTH.

This is what strategically becomes your flag.

When creating your offers, what you sell, when you go speak in front of an audience, when you introduce yourself on a podcast, this is the PURPOSE ALL YOUR WORK SERVES... This is WHY you do what you do.

When you're describing your services, your core truth is the reason you created them.

Here's an (my) example:

My core truth is that YOU ARE UNIQUE and that we do not need to fabricate your brand, it already exists we just need to uncover it. The more YOU, you become, the more UNIQUE your business becomes and attracts the right people. YOU just need to be known for what you want to be known and grow your audience with YOUR message, followed by an offer that makes sense for the person you want to serve.

So each of my offers from this book (born in my Ascension mastermind program) to my Be You Brand Academy (a year-long business program focused on building a profitable personal brand) to my live events - EVERYTHING serves that purpose, to help women uncover their uniqueness, get clarity in their messaging, and bring it to the world in the way of a profitable personal brand that can change the world one person at a time.

I know, from working with hundreds of women, THERE IS A REASON you do what you do OVER DOING SOMETHING ELSE.

The Ripple Effect

For example, my client, Stephanie, is a Personal Growth Coach. She helps women go after the life they truly want, not the life "they think they are supposed to want."

When she came to me, she used to be a very successful realtor, but at some point, she realized that job was what "she was supposed to do." She made a lot of money and she had a good reputation. From the outside looking in, it looked amazing. You'd think she should have been happy, but she wasn't.

So she started looking at her life and doing personal development.

She looked deep into herself and she realized she was living by everyone else's rules. Simply put, she was doing what "society" told her should make her happy, and eventually, she kicked the board... She adopted a little girl. She moved states, and after changing her own life and finding her path, she started a new business helping women with their mental health and those just like her who are pursuing the life they WANT. A life of fulfillment whatever that means to THEM...

Do you see the crux here…?

She saw a need, she had a visceral experience with that need herself.

And SHE WANTED TO PASS IT ALONG.

Yes, of course, she wants to make money, and she must do so, that is how she will impact more women. She would not be able to stay in the game if she did this for free.

It is a business after all, but that does not make it less meaningful (let's start normalizing people getting paid for the amazing work they do, which is equally fulfilling and profitable!).

If you are a business owner, most likely, you had a similar experience.

So, you're probably saying, okay, Ati, what does this have to do with changing the world?

Here's the thing … There are a million coaches.

A million therapists (Steph is also getting her therapy license).

A million women are doing "the same," but the way she is bringing it out is through her unique approach and her unique character. It cannot and would never be able to be replicated… even if someone wanted to. BECAUSE THEY ARE NOT STEPH.

This is a fact for every single one of us. And you.

The key to this? Truly sourcing from the inside. Truly listening to our thoughts and reflecting on what we truly believe to be the truth.

Why is this important?

Because we are all part of the big collective… and in every industry, we are helping people with problems that, at the end of the day, WILL ENHANCE their lives as a whole (one person at a time).

When people's problems are fewer or disappear, they live better lives.

When people live better lives, they are happier.

When people are happier, wealthier, healthier, WE ALL WIN.

THE WORLD WINS…

Let me prove it to you.

My big truth is EVERY SINGLE ONE OF YOU IS UNIQUE AND HAS A TRUTH, and that is the reason you started your business… You chose THIS BUSINESS although you could be doing ANYTHING ELSE. But you are not. You are pursuing THIS PASSION.

BUT… I believe after seeing so many women do this (including myself), we self-censor.

We doubt.

We are scared to "offend others."

We have BAGGAGE.

For many reasons.

The way we grew up.

Society.

Our own limiting beliefs.

I believe in my core that when we overcome this, we can succeed.

Women like us have big dreams, but usually, we belong to one of the following groups:

1. The ones that never go for it and live with regret and what-ifs.
2. The ones that go for it, but don't fully believe they have something "special" to offer, are watering themselves down. (Women in this group usually can grow a business, somewhat successfully, but not to their fullest potential.)

3. The group that believes they HAVE SOMETHING AMAZING, they are passionate and they are living in their power, and changing the world one client/woman at a time. (Usually, this group was group 2 at some point.)

No matter which group you belong to right now, know that if you have the calling of being made for more, you can achieve more. But you must first believe in yourself.

Back in 2019, I was the woman in Group 2.

It's like there was a glass between who I knew I could be and who I was being.

I was scared.

I cried often.

I had a story in my mind that I was not a smart businesswoman (this was the recurrent story I would tell myself without even knowing).

I didn't know how to attract business to me.

And honestly, I had a hard time seeing success through all of that.

I was not living up to my potential.

When a woman is not living up to her full potential, what do you think she is modeling to her children?

The same fears.

The same stories.

That staying small is a safer way of thinking.

And I know, you don't want your kids to play "small," do you? You wouldn't let your best friend play small, would you? You would call her out!

Can you see the ripple effect here…

Not only that… think about this…

Imagine if I stayed in the scared mindset in 2019... Hundreds of women maybe would have never pursued building their brand, their businesses, and going after their dreams...

Imagine if my client Steph had never actually changed careers and helped the women she is helping...

Some of those women may have never actually changed their lives...

That is the ripple effect: that is the power of the collective, that is the POWER OF STEPPING INTO YOUR POWER.

The world is made up of problems needing to be solved daily... whatever you are called to help the world with... is POWERFUL.

It is YOUR contribution to the collective. It is your contribution to the WORLD, that cannot be minimized. The world is changed by the crazy ones.

I know if you are here... you are (one of the crazy ones) in the right place at the right time.

And the world needs you. When you help one person, and another, and another... that is when we see real change. We cannot change the BIG things in the world (unless you go into politics, and that is not my cup of tea, lol), but most of us are agents of change in our backyards, in our neighborhoods, in our communities.

And let's be even more truthful, you will work with way more than 3 clients in your life, so think of the ripple effect that has on the world.

That, my friend, is MY TRUTH: YOUR "BE YOU BRAND" POWER MESSAGE is yours and only yours. It is already inside you, it just needs to be discovered and nurtured. Nobody can do it like you do and my genius is to help you bring it out to the world, amplify it, make it magnetic, and monetize it. What is your genius?

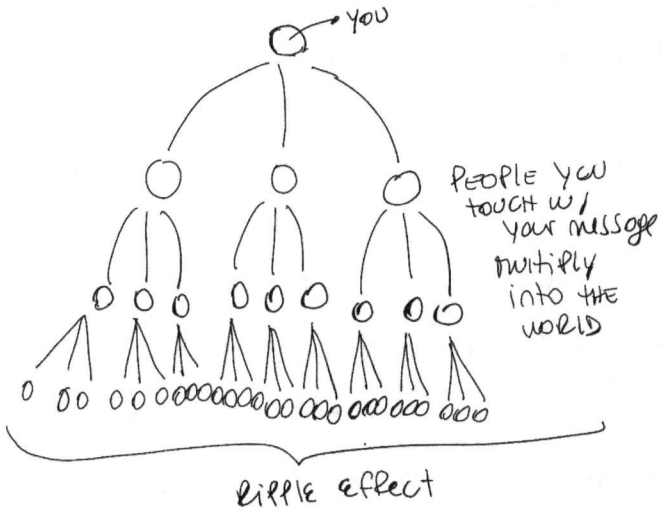

ripple effect

This book was born of the same "need": helping women find their genius in telling their stories. It has been an agent of change for the women in it in so many ways, and it has not even been published yet (although it will be by the time you read it).

Our stories and unique experiences are key to how and why we do things differently.

That is why it is so important that after you acquire a skill, you "sift" it through YOU.

That you get the courage to do YOU with it.

The Framework

Here is the framework I use with my clients to help them gain insight into their geniuses, find their authenticity within what they do, and gain clarity.

Phase 1: ASSESS

Assess where you are when it comes to your core truth and your reputation.

Do you know what it is? Have you identified your core truth? Your why?

We assess how you see yourself and how others see you.

ACTION STEP: Ask a few people in your circle:

"What three things come to mind when you think of me?"

You will do this on social media, AND text 3–5 people around you.

This should be people in your circle of influence when it comes to your business or what you are building your brand around.

The important part here is that you use your common sense. If Auntie Susie answers with "blond curls from when you were 3 years old," that is not necessarily the answer you are looking for, nor is she probably the right person to ask.

Beware: How long you have been doing what you do plays a part. If you just started your business, it will be a great indicator of how well you are doing at letting people know WHAT YOU DO.

If you have been at it for a while, the same applies.

It is a great baseline and feedback to mark the progress you are making and the effectiveness of your efforts. It is also great at gauging what people think of you, especially things that you might miss. Because again, we are who we are, and we are not always aware of how people perceive us.

When you do this on social media, post to your feed, to your stories, and tag me! I always love seeing people doing this exercise [tag at @atig.branding on Instagram]

Phase 2: SELF-DISCOVERY

This is the tip of the iceberg.

This is your Brand self-discovery process. You may think you started for the money or the freedom, but there is a DEEPER LEVEL. (There always is.)

This is an inward process, not an outward one.

Many women spend years looking outwards. And that is one of the reasons they never find clarity.

The message is inside of you, not on the outside.

However, the potency of this message comes down not only to "just" discovering it, but also stepping into your power, embodying it, living it, spreading it, and really understanding YOU and your point of view. BELIEVE IT WILL CHANGE LIVES.

It sounds easier than it is. We live in a world where social media bombards us daily, so staying true to your views can be quite challenging. Here is an important truth: If you are worried you will offend someone… you are molding your truth to them and that is ultimately hurting your ability to help the collective and the mission you are here to fulfill.

Why do you do what you do, as opposed to doing anything else? Take this question seriously and GO ALL OUT. Do not hold back.

Once you have this question flushed out, you are ready to find your authentic brand.

Phase 3: Discover Your TRUE Authenticity

This is the contemplation phase.

The next exercise is a set of questions every woman who is the face of her brand (if you are a service provider, this is you 100%) should ask herself to show up authentically and embed her truth into everything she does.

Note: This process can be done each time your views evolve, change, or you lose clarity. You and your business will evolve, and some of this may evolve with you. AND THAT IS OK.

To stay true to yourself and always grow with your core desires and message, we recommend doing this exercise at least once a year, twice if you are in hyper-growth.

While this is still part of your self-discovery, having phases 1–2 done is crucial. You cannot know what your authentic point of view is if you haven't dug into your transformation and WHY YOU DO WHAT YOU DO.

My advice is that you do this exercise all in one sitting. Let your answers flow freely, find your center, and take a deep breath before starting - so you are grounded on your big why. Do not overthink this…

1. What made you decide to offer the service(s) you offer? (What was your experience with your service? This could have been a gap that you experienced and wished existed, a struggle you went through... It is your story.)
2. What does success mean to you? Forget about "shoulds," this is about you and your truest self, and your thoughts.
3. To become an authority in your field, you have to establish your expertise - What are 3 topics you could teach right now to demonstrate this knowledge? What can you talk and talk and talk about because you ARE OBSESSED WITH IT?
4. What are 3 adjectives you would like to EVOKE through your content? For example, mine are fun, unapologetic, positive, and growth.
5. What are the things in your industry that DRIVE YOU CRAZY, that you don't agree with, OR that you see a GAP in? THIS IS CRUCIAL for you to lean into.

6. Decide what is important to you. For example, do you mind showing up with or without makeup? Is this going to stop you from showing up if you are busy one day? Decide now how you will show up when doubt arises. This will become your guiding force. As an expert in this realm, I recommend mixing up how you show up online, having a mix of curated and non-curated images, stories, and videos so people can relate to you.

7. What do you stand for? What are topics you would like to incorporate into your platform related or unrelated to business?

8. How much of your personal life do you want to share? What is relevant to your client? For example: if you are a relationship coach, showing snippets of your marriage may be necessary. For me, as a personal brand coach, that may not be relevant. As a health coach, showing your breakfast may be relevant but not showing your relationship. Get clarity by asking yourself, what do I want to share, and WHY? This will bring you so much freedom about not being glued to your social media daily while showing up strategically.

(Download the companion for a full set of guiding questions and an Authenticity "challenge" at https://atigbranding.myflodesk.com/bybbook)

The beautiful part about getting real with your authenticity is that you truly get to find yourself. You get to fulfill your purpose and make a difference in the world for others. WIN-WIN.

This next part was a pivotal moment in my journey - a realization that changed everything for me in one second:

"In my mind's eye, I saw my little 8-year-old self, holding the imaginary mic, wearing a little white dress, dancing in front of the mirror, hands up in pure joy dancing, and I remembered who she was…"

This wasn't just a memory. It was a profound reconnection with my authentic self, helping me overcome my self-doubt and rediscover my passion.

I saw this in 2023, on stage, hosting my own women's event, looking at the 80 women who attended changing their lives right in front of my eyes.

These prompts, I shared with you, this same discovery process, are the ones I have been using with myself (and my clients) as I KEEP EVOLVING AND STEPPING INTO MY POWER. Growing. And helping women BELIEVE in themselves. And tell their stories.

It was through another chapter in another book that my transformation began. It was so cathartic that I knew I wanted to hold the same space for women.

The Ati from 2019 would have NOT believed she had it in her to host an international conference, gather women, write a book together, and INSPIRE them to tell their stories.

BE SURE to not confuse the beginning of your story with someone else's middle.

ALLOW yourself to have your story, your growth, your evolution. No matter where that is right now, it is yours and it is beautifully unfolding.

I often remind myself of this too; because we never stop growing, we never stop having fears, and the fears only evolve. And new ones appear.

The Power of Stepping Up

If you get one thing from this book, STEP INTO YOUR POWER, NEVER PLAY SMALL AGAIN. When you play small, out of fear, doubt, and people-pleasing, EVERYONE LOSES, including yourself.

You have the power to change the world by being unapologetically YOU. Embrace your truth, share your story, and let your unique light shine. Together, we can create a ripple effect of positive change bigger than what we ever thought possible.

If anyone knows that, it's this former bartender, turned photographer, turned coach, turned speaker, turned writer. Turned everything she desired to become, and still going.

Not because anyone anointed her. But because she leaned into her authentic desires and core truth. THAT WE ARE ALL UNIQUE AND AMAZING IN OUR OWN WAY. And that includes you.

"Authenticity doesn't automatically guarantee success, but inauthenticity guarantees failure."
Jamie Kern Lima

Let's recap how you can do this work, right away:

TAP INTO YOUR AUTHENTICITY

Because we all know how it goes… you will read the book and do nothing with it, and we don't want that, do we?

1. **Self-Assessment**: How do you see yourself, and how do others see you?
2. **Self-Discovery**: Looking inward. Why?
3. **Contemplation**: Where it gets real, ask yourself the right questions.

My desire for you is that you love yourself for everything you are, accept yourself for everything you are not, and work toward becoming everything you desire to be.

Expand your awareness and BRING MORE OF WHO YOU ALREADY ARE INTO WHAT YOU DO.

If you are ready to go deep, download the companion guide for a full set of guiding questions to help you on your journey: https://atigbranding.myflodesk.com/bybbook

No journey has grown me more (so far) than becoming a mother, a business owner, a coach, and a speaker. Loving every one of my clients and lovingly helping them shine.

Love, light, and be your brand vibes. Cheers to unapologetically being you 100% of the time!

Ati Grinspun

Next Steps to stay connected with us.

- **Join the Community**: Connect with like-minded women in the BE YOU BRAND Academy to continue your journey of self-discovery and brand building inside our Personal Brand Strategies for Female Entrepreneurs FB group.
- **Stay Inspired**: Follow me on social media @ati.g.branding for daily inspiration, practical tips, and success stories.
- **Tune In**: Listen to our podcast for deeper insights and personal stories.
- **Share Your Journey**: Share your thoughts and experiences with us! Tag us on Instagram @atigbranding with your stories of self-discovery and brand building.
- **Join the Mastermind**: Join the next round of Ascension Mastermind to write your Anthology with a group of like-minded women. Email Ati@atigrinspun.com for full mastermind info.

Jeanette Cefre

Conngage
Business Activation Coach & Mentor

https://www.linkedin.com/in/jeanette-cefre/
https://www.instagram.com/conn_gage/

After 30+ years in the corporate world of travel tech, Jeanette found her blueprint for life taking an unexpected yet fulfilling turn. Corporate life was stable, rewarding, and she even managed to carve her own niche of expertise without a formal degree. Her self-taught skills and innovative approaches elevated her responsibilities, but one thing truly gave her a sense of purpose: helping women be seen.

When the pandemic shook the foundations of companies globally, Jeanette saw it as a chance to realign her life's blueprint. She left her corporate role and dove into her passion for helping female solopreneurs. Conquering her own fears and self-doubt, she committed to guiding women on their first steps in entrepreneurship.

As a Content Activation Coach and Mentor, Jeanette helps women solopreneurs overcome content creation barriers, develop sustainable systems, and enhance their visibility. Her mission is to increase the number of successful women entrepreneurs globally.

Unlikely

By Jeanette Cefre

It was unlikely a Filipina girl from Guam was going to change the world. I'm a Libra, after all, and I can't even decide between Speculoos cookies or coffee ice cream. It's surreal to me that the decisions I made a few years ago put me on the road that led me to this life—my second life. A life which existed only in dreams and my journals. The irony? I only found this life because I was so lost.

The Expectation

I'll start my story with some context.

It's a stereotype I know, but being a Filipina, the blueprint for me was to be a nurse. My immediate circle was filled with Filipina nurses and they shared the same benefits over and over again: You can find work anywhere in the world, it's good pay, if you work hard you can be head nurse, you can specialize in something you really like, it's secure, etc.

And, for the most part, I was sold. I mean, who wouldn't be with all those benefits. If I'm being honest, I wanted to be a nurse because it would make my parents unbelievably proud. It meant I would've gone to university (as they only had an 8th-grade education). It meant they could say to their family, friends or strangers - with pride, "My daughter is a nurse."

As per the blueprint, I was to graduate high school with flying colors so I could get into the best nursing program. I was on track. I did what other kids did as a freshman, I started researching what I needed to "get into" the school of my choice. Three years seemed far away and I didn't think about my plans any further than that. I also did what other kids did, that is, skip school, go to parties, have a boyfriend, work and study in between.

I applied to an accelerated nursing program that would allow me to reach my goal in just two years and thankfully I was accepted. I attended nursing school during the day and worked the late shift for an airline on the reservation desk (yup, you had to call a number to make an airline reservation). It was an entry-level position, but it was my first corporate job. Not only was the blueprint in motion, I was one year ahead of schedule.

What I didn't realize was, in the coming months, my life would not be the same.

Due to a heavy workload at nursing school, I missed a lot of work. It wasn't long before I was fired for too many absences. What now? I had bills to pay – school, a car note, insurance, etc. I wasn't really worried, because I knew I could find another job. The problem? Telling my parents that I no longer had one, especially since my father worked for the same company. They would be disappointed and I would've brought shame on the family by getting fired. What would they say to the family, friends or strangers who asked? It was all too embarrassing. I didn't tell them. I just couldn't. I kept up appearances by going to school during the day and then just hanging out at my boyfriend's house and looking for jobs.

From there it was a downward spiral, in terms of the blueprint because I definitely wasn't prepared for what happened next.

Down, down, down

I got pregnant. I was almost 3 months along when I found out. It wasn't uncommon for me not to have a regular cycle, and I had no other indications (eating more, gaining weight, etc.) that I was. At this point, there was no turning back. I deferred from my nursing program with the hopes of returning one day. My thoughts turned to my parents. If I couldn't tell them about getting fired, how in the world would I tell them I'm pregnant?

The realization set in that in 6 months, I would be a parent and a mother, without a degree or job. All at 19 years old.

I went from following the blueprint to being lost.

It was from this moment on where I stopped thinking and looking into the future. I felt I was in survival mode. This would be the theme of my life for a very long time.

Thankfully, I found a job with a major cruise line. I was able to tell my parents I found a new job making sure to highlight the positives - better salary, benefits, location, etc. Whew! I also told them that I deferred the remaining time for the nursing program due to the hours of this job. They weren't happy, but they accepted it.

At the time, I lived with my parents, I mean, I was 19. Naturally I was home more because I didn't have school and I had a 9-5 job.

Sitting at the table having breakfast one morning, my mother asks me, "Are you pregnant?"

Reflex answer, "No. What makes you say that?"

As mothers do, she goes down this list of how my body shape has changed. I'm just lying around the house, I'm more sensitive, and there are no signs of my period. After lying my ass off for an hour, I had to go to work. I thought that was the end of that. Little did I know I was going to spiral down even further.

It all happened so fast. I came back home that evening and in my room was a pregnancy test. Of course it came out positive. She had to tell my dad. He told me to get out of his house and to leave the car they had bought for me.

In 5 months time, I would be a parent, a mother, have no degree, no car and homeless. All at 19 years old. At least I had an income.

Lost like never before

At that point, I had to live with my boyfriend. We played house for a while, but that is also the time where things between us changed.

My belly seemed to have popped out of nowhere. As it grew, I saw him less and less, even though we lived together. He was working, hanging out with his friends and going to clubs to party. The time we did spend together was full of arguments that led to fights which led him to be out of the house more. To fill the empty space both emotionally and physically, I poured myself into romantic thoughts about the future with my baby.

My life imploded when I came home early from work one day. I wasn't feeling well and needed to rest. I walked into the house and I saw my boyfriend's best friend there, but no sign of my boyfriend. "What are you doing here and where is he?" I asked.

He looked at me with pity and all he could say was "I'm sorry Jeanette. I don't want to get in the middle."

My boyfriend didn't have a car so he borrowed his best friend's car and I knew exactly where he was and I drove straight to *her* house.

My heart was racing as I walked up to the door and rang the doorbell. He answered it, and we started arguing. He tells me to leave because he won't be. Devastated, I went back home, ransacked his room, and then I called my mom and begged her to let me come home.

In 3 months time, I will be a parent, a mother, have no degree, and cheated on while I was pregnant. All at 19 years old. At least I had an income and at least I wasn't homeless.

A few days later, I started bleeding. My doctor said I needed to go to the hospital immediately. I couldn't drive. My mother didn't drive. My sister was only 12. My dad wasn't there. I had no other choice but to call my ex. Don't ask me why I didn't call 911, I don't remember.

He came to bring me to the hospital, but he brought "her." As the tears rolled down my face, all my mom and sister could do was console me and tell me it would be okay.

I'm now a single parent, a mother, have no degree, and no boyfriend. All at 19 years old. At least I had an income and my daughter who would love me.

It was unlikely I would fulfill the blueprint. It was unlikely I could make my parents proud in the way they expected. It was unlikely that the road would be a straight line. It didn't matter because it was no longer about me. My official degree would be in motherhood.

The Entrepreneurial Spirit

I stayed with the cruise line until they let me go. I found other jobs in customer service, but they didn't pay well. I was living from check to check, but I made it work. As long as I had a salary to pay my bills and health insurance, I thought I was winning. However, I was tired of robbing Peter to pay Paul and always on the lookout for ways to save or make additional money.

Then, I found Avon. I loved their affordable products and was intrigued by a coworker selling Avon as a side-hustle. Curious about her earnings and effort, she sold me the dream of having more money and my own business. "Sign me up!" I said.

I did it for six months. I didn't meet quotas, made no profit, and my upline abandoned me because I wasn't contributing. Despite this, the MLM (multi-level marketing) bug got me, and I also sold Mary Kay Cosmetics and Creative Memories Scrapbooking Systems over the next few years.

Nothing stuck. It was Avon all over again, with products taking up space in my house that no one wanted to buy. It was unlikely I'd succeed in MLM, so I kept trying to find better opportunities in the corporate world.

What did stick was my willingness to try and the idea that I could have something of my own. I learned that without leadership truly invested in your success, it takes much longer to achieve your goals.

The Corporate Life

I managed to stay in the travel industry and leaned more towards travel tech. I ended up finding a company that I grew up with for the next 27 years. This became my university to which I would earn my "experiential professional" degree.

I wore many hats all around the customer service domain. I went from a customer service representative to customer service team lead. From there, I became an Instructional Designer (aka teacher) and that is where my passion for teaching came from. My last role in the corporate world was like a Swiss Army Knife as it truly encapsulated 27+ years in corporate. I was the Learning, Knowledge, and Community Manager and Head of Internal Communication for my division. (Wow, writing that is so weird). It was truly a dream job, I loved it, and was even passionate about it.

Over time, I was the go-to person for all things learning, knowledge management, communication and best of all innovative ideas. When it came to looking for new concepts, new ways of doing things, I was usually pulled into the conversation. I was known for pushing the boundaries of what can be done "in a corporate environment." I took what existed outside of the corporate world, adapted it, and made it work inside.

"Me, have my own logo that
one day people will recognize? Nah."

I didn't set out to have a particular identity or personal brand, nor did I even think about this concept. My perception of a brand was that only big companies with thousands of employees selling a product or service could have a brand, not me. I was, however, making an impact in my own way. Little did I know, I had created my own, personal brand.

Thing is, I was unfulfilled. I felt like a great white shark in a fish tank. I had the potential to grow into something magnificent but was limited by my environment. I had occupied the space as much as I could. I didn't have a recognized degree and that is what determined your base salary and upward movement in the company. Although I was already working for the company for 20+ years, my salary only went up by 2% each year with the potential for a bonus. Each time the yearly review came, I was hopeful but had low expectations of major changes. They say that your age should be the gauge for your salary. I can tell you that my age was always higher.

It was VERY unlikely I would advance further than where I was, so I continued being an amazing corporate citizen.

Moments of What If

I kept a journal and every once in a while feelings of "ugh" would surface. Feelings of knowing I can contribute so much more. Perhaps in a different context. Perhaps in a less structured, more open environment. There were a lot of sentences that began with "I wish." Then other parts of my journal were occupied with ideas. Those were defining moments as they kept a candle burning for whatever was there. At the time, I didn't know what it was, but it was there. One of those moments was when I helped a friend with her transition to entrepreneurship.

She worked in the same company and a life change put her on the path to entrepreneurship. She became vegan and she was in the process of leaving corporate to become a vegan chef. When she was putting her business plan together, she asked me to look at what she had created in terms of her brand, specifically the name of the company and her visual identity. Several working lunches later, we landed on something she seriously considered. I was shocked and happy when she told me she went with the name I suggested and the font for her logo. That feeling of helping her get to the next step was amazing. At that moment, I thought, "Wouldn't it be great to help women start their businesses and I can help them with stuff like this"?

Another entry in my journal included possible names of the business I would never have. They included: Third Eye Consulting, Idea Storming and Simply Jeanette Cefre.

Most journal entries ended with "someday."

It was unlikely I would have a business because I didn't see myself as having one.

Endings and beginnings

The pandemic hit. Companies worldwide were reducing staff and we were all scared. In an effort to not go through this painful exercise, the company created a voluntary leave package. You could apply for this package under three conditions: pre-retirement, taking over a business or starting your own business.

I was neither close to pre-retirement or owning a business. Despite all the ideas my journal had, owning a business never crossed my mind. I deleted the email.

In parallel, my marriage, which was hanging on by a thread for the last 10 years, was ending. With the isolation of the pandemic and being alone for the first time in 20+ years, I felt lost, again.

It was a Sunday in August 2020. I invited my then husband to lunch. We had been officially separated for one year but emotionally separated for longer (that's another book). The pandemic taught all of us that life was short, and it was time to cut the cord. During lunch, we discussed what was happening with the voluntary leave (he worked at the same company too). He then said to me, "You know, you will never have an opportunity like this again. You have worked for the company for 27 years, and you will have enough resources to do what you have been thinking about. Why not go for it"?

I immediately rejected the idea. I spewed out all the reasons why it couldn't work. "I don't know anything about business." "It's probably so hard to get the entrepreneur license." "I'm not a salesperson." "I suck at math, can you imagine having to do my taxes, budget, etc." I mean, I didn't even give it a chance.

I quickly switched gears to the topic of divorce. "I want a divorce." He said, "Okay."

With one conversation, we ended our 20 year marriage in the same village where we started our life in France together. I walked away not thinking about life without him, but thoughts about starting my business.

I went for it.

And while I felt it was unlikely to be approved, it was.

Trials and Tribulations of Entrepreneurship

I knew the first thing I needed to do was to develop my brand. After scouring the internet, I found a **free** master class, Be You Brand. Wow, what a wealth of information! I felt it was the roadmap I needed to get to my destination. This master class answered most of the questions I had. It was such a relief to find someone who could coach me toward my purpose. Someone who was a leader, who walked the walk and showed up not only for herself, but for others. In the first strategy call with her, she identified that I needed to pivot and do something I was aligned with. It was then I realized that, without knowing it, I'd built my brand in corporate. I didn't have to start from scratch, I had already built a foundation and needed to leverage it.

Whew, what a relief. For the first time in over 20 years, I felt hopeful.

I knew there would be challenges, but I was ready for it. It wasn't long before the reality of entrepreneurship started to creep up and expose all my vulnerable areas.

The unexpected challenge I had was mindset. It was a biggie! The first mindset barrier I had was shifting from employee to entrepreneur. After over 30 years in corporate life, I was used to the structure already being there. I just showed up and did my part. As a solopreneur, I'm the CEO - Chief Everything Officer - so I have to do all the parts which include building that structure. On paper I was an entrepreneur, however my other barriers like low self-esteem, people pleasing, and a perfectionist (disguised as a procrastinator) didn't allow me to embody it. I was stuck in the employee mindset.

I was overwhelmed, and lacking both clarity and confidence. Not only that, my money mindset was not a positive one. Growing up, I was told we didn't have any money so I shouldn't ask or want things and to be grateful for what I had. My interpretation was that to think abundantly felt wrong or selfish, much less ask to be abundant. Scarcity became my default thought around money and all my decisions were made from that place.

After 1.5 years without making any significant revenue, I panicked and considered going back to corporate and started to look for a job. I applied for almost 100 jobs and got only 10 responses and 2 interviews. Yeah, right. I was screwed. What have I done?

A month after my dismal attempt to find a job, I landed a 5-figure consulting opportunity. It was the proof I needed. I gave entrepreneurship another chance.

Pivoting, again

The inner voice telling me to go back to corporate is ever present. Some days it's stronger than others. It never really leaves me. It's just dormant until a situation awakens it. Case in point.

After 2 years of being an entrepreneur and a couple of thousand dollars down, I was lost, again. It's what I do, bounce between clarity and "what the fuck am I doing." Aside from current obligations, I did nothing for 1.5 almost 2 months. The most I could do was watch true crime documentaries and play games on my phone. In between, I questioned everything. I couldn't understand why I wasn't where I needed to be in terms of my business.

> *What I didn't realize is that people saw my genius when I couldn't see it. It was something that I felt was so effortless to me, so I thought it was effortless to everyone.*

What has kept me in my entrepreneurial spirit so far is that I'm surrounded by people who hold the space for me, even when I can't see the light at the end of the tunnel.

After completing the program in the Be You Brand Academy, my coach asked me to be part of her team as a Tech and Content Peer Coach. My role was to help them apply what they've learned in the courses to their business. She always told me this was my strength and my "zone of genius" but I honestly didn't think so. I was just being me.

Knowing I was in a low place, my accountability peer coach asked, "why don't you do what you do for the Be You Brand Academy?"

I swear, the light bulb came on. Could I? Should I?

This meant another pivot in my short entrepreneurial life. The first was when I left corporate to become a Virtual Event Strategist. My second pivot was to be a Business Activation Coach and Mentor helping women transition to entrepreneurship from corporate to get their business started. Now, here's my third pivot – I'm a Content Activation Coach and Mentor helping female solopreneurs overcome content creation barriers leading them to visibility breakthroughs. Together we create sustainable systems and processes that leverage their natural way of working enabling them to show up consistently and be seen by their ideal clients.

So what's different? It feels natural. I light up when I talk about this topic. All the insights I gained in the various roles I had in corporate have led me to this point. In fact, it's almost the same with a different audience. Learning and development taught me to hone in on a client's real need. Knowledge management sharpened my skills to connect the dots in order to build effective systems and processes. Community management has given me specific insights into what a community needs to thrive.

Finding Myself

I'll be honest, I overcomplicated my personal brand. There are many formulas out there on how to craft your brand, and I've tried many of them. Truth is, they only serve as guides.

I learned that your brand means nothing if you can't embody it authentically. You've got to lean into what you naturally do and use that as the foundation of your brand. Defining your brand becomes challenging when you're not aligned with who you are. And in entrepreneurship, being who you are is not optional; it's absolutely mandatory.

Entrepreneurship helped me figure out who I am. In hindsight, I was never really lost. Those unlikely events in my life created the path I needed to take to be where and who I am today. Becoming a young mother made me resilient and strong. Dabbling in MLMs early on revealed my entrepreneurial spirit. Being at my lowest point forced me to trust myself and do what I do best.

I want to challenge you to confront your own fears, dreams, and vulnerabilities. Embrace what you know you are great at and accept it as your "zone of genius." What would it look like if you not only worked on the barriers but actually made a breakthrough? Would it mean achieving something you never thought you could?

The only thing between a barrier and a breakthrough is the first step towards overcoming it.

To help you take that first step, I've created a free downloadable to help you find your "flow." Here, you'll discover the 5 foundational elements that will help you overcome barriers preventing you from being seen by your ideal client. This resource will guide you in aligning with your authentic self, so you can show up consistently and confidently.

Thank you for being part of my journey. I share my story in hopes you'll consider that having feelings of being lost or "unlikely" are part of something bigger. Listen to your intuition and those nudges you've been receiving because they just may lead you to the life you've always wanted.

Amber Voigt

Owner of Ennoble

https://www.linkedin.com/in/amber-voigt-439178165/
https://www.facebook.com/profile.php?id=100005431726977
https://www.instagram.com/ennoble_transformation/
https://www.ennobleadv.com/lander

Amber Voigt is a widely recognized expert in Insurance, Sales/Service, Marketing Strategies, Entrepreneurship, Leadership and Management Development and, Business Strategies and Implementation with appearances on Unburden Your Business Podcast, 101 Business Network and more, commencing her career in 1999 at the time when she was only 19 years old.

Today, when she's not working on her businesses or helping other entrepreneurs you will find her nose in a book, on a plane, cooking a plant based meal, meditating or with her family.

You'll often observe Amber helping small business owners with their marketing and business processes. She loves nothing more than seeing other go-getters elevate their businesses to the top of their industries.

For further insights into Amber Voigt and the ways she can support you in business growth through processes and marketing, explore her expertise at www.ennobleadv.com.

Power of Pivot

By Amber Voigt

A five-hour flight changed my life, and I've been earning my wings ever since…

Here I was again alone, afraid, and unsure of the future. Sitting in my window seat staring out into the dark, I caught a glimpse of myself in the reflection. Only I could see the pain, fear, and loneliness in them. I whispered to myself over and over, "Say goodbye, you are not going that way anymore." Little did I know that this flight leaving the life I knew in New Jersey at 17 years old would be the first of many transformations and pivots for me. As the wheels hit the ground in Colorado, I caught one final glance at myself. This time there was a determined edge to the eyes staring back at me. Somehow I was transformed with a new sense of confidence and power reminding me that this was the first of many life-changing discoveries to come.

The drive from the airport to my new home was one of complete darkness with each mile getting darker as we got further away from the city. I had never been to where I was heading, but I knew it was a beginning. I prayed nonstop during that drive that this would be a better life than the one I left behind.

Sleep came easy that first night, and waking up the next morning to finally see my surroundings affirmed my decision. The house was on top of a hill in the foothills. On one side all I could see were the Rocky Mountains, which demanded full attention in their presence alone. As I turned to absorb the awe and beauty around me I saw land going for miles with horses and an abundance of green. Looking south, you could glimpse an area that was inviting you to explore further. I must have stood there in utter wonder for hours. I had never felt freedom before and I swear it still feels like blue skies, sunshine, and wide open spaces to me. The world looked huge as I gazed in each direction. The sun felt different on my skin, I felt different, I was different.

Everything was different, but most noticeably I was different; it didn't happen overnight, but looking back it feels like that was the moment I took control of my life and realized I had to make the choices and decisions instead of others. Up until that point, my life was full of packing, partying, days of silence, moving, saying goodbye to best friends, and praying for new ones. Each day shaky and unsure. I would look around for solid ground and only find sand beneath me full of uncertainties, heartbreak, and insecurities. I was an only child and often felt like everything was on my shoulders, never having the confidence or wisdom to know how to handle my inner emotions or how to make good decisions. The only point of reference I lived by was if everyone around me approved or felt happy within themselves. I only felt ok if those around me were happy and content. Little did I know, the constant seeking of approval chipped away at my soul, losing more and more of myself with each yes I tried to give each mask I had to put on and take off. It got to the point of deciding to just do everything that came my way and deal with the consequences later, of which there were many. I caused a lot of pain, chaos, and wreckage by not knowing myself or being true to who I was created to be. I became desperate, feeling as if I had no voice of my own. Pretending to have it all under control is a lonely and dangerous path to be on.

Standing on that hill in Colorado was the first day I saw the world as a wonderful place full of freedom and possibilities. I could be whoever I wanted from that moment and that person was my true self, that's who I wanted to be, and I could feel I was exactly in the place I needed to be for it to happen. It became the first step of many to transformation, growth, and strength. You see, the beginning of any change is seeing things differently, seeing yourself in a different light. Even the air around me was different, with every breath I could feel myself being filled and refreshed with ideas, desires, and possibilities. With each exhale I felt the weight of past uncertainty leaving me, expelling the uncertainties of my life along with every poor choice I had ever made to that point. I didn't know what was coming for me next, but I decided my life would never be the same. In reflection, I realize that many small steps turn into a life and it was up to me to decide if it was one of struggle and failure or one of success and ultimately victory.

Growing up I tried to surround myself with as many friends as I could, especially boyfriends. I was always alone in my room at home and I longed to be connected somewhere, anywhere. I held on to people and unhealthy choices just for the idea of being loved and wanted. What I really wanted was to love myself. That 5-hour flight opened the door for me. I was more alone than ever but finally listening to my own voice and desires. I did everything by myself. I drove on the windy roads with the windows down singing songs I chose, went to eat, and shopped at places I wanted to. I became who I wanted to be all by myself. In a few months, I started meeting people and felt the confidence to say no if I didn't feel a healthy connection. I no longer partied, sought others' approval, or sacrificed my true self for the sake of others. I started reading and enjoyed people who were driven, successful, and mature with a passion for talking about important things like growth, goals, struggles, and contemplating the world around us.

It wasn't long before the shaky ground I had always known turned into a solid path. I had grown to trust myself. I had a vision and the determination to see it through. Having air to finally breathe and people around me that poured into my soul, allowed dreams to form and love to blossom. One of those people became my future husband. A man that supported, appreciated, and loved the true, honest, and real me for me. Together we built a solid foundation allowing our entrepreneurial dreams to become a reality. The risks taken were methodical and calculated, not reckless. I was in a place of confidence, surrounded by an encouraging network of family and friends. I knew and more importantly, expected there would be peaks and valleys coming my way but I was truly ready to face them head-on.

It was easy to think I had it all together after coming so far in such a short time. If anyone from New Jersey had run into me they would never recognize the person I had become. The new version stood tall, had opinions and strength, and couldn't be swayed against her convictions. I was content standing on my own. The first big test came at 18 with a positive pregnancy test. I would be lying if I said I wasn't rattled. I stared at that test and all the fears and insecurities rushed through my system. I looked at myself in the mirror and saw a child. Yes, I had overcome so much and grown into a person I was proud of, but being a mom? I was still teaching myself. I splashed water on my face, took three deep breaths, and squared my shoulders. I spoke to that frightened face in the mirror and told her, "You aren't alone and even if you are, it is enough." I walked out of that bathroom, told Jason and he reacted with the biggest smile and excitement. It was the first time I took immediate action and faced something hard straight on. This was new, this was what being transformed over the past few months meant.

The fears and obstacles changed over the years but each one was met with the same approach - acknowledgement, reflection, and resilience. By my mid-twenties, we had worked together in a family business of pool halls for years. Shortly after our second daughter was born we realized pool halls were no longer in line with the lives we wanted for our family. It was time to transition into a more stable and family-friendly lifestyle. Once again we were faced with change and decisions that had to be made. For us, that meant a drive across the country to get some perspective and dreams in our souls. Through each mile, we searched within, saw a different and better life, laughed, had the windows down, and belted out our favorite songs. When we pulled back into Colorado, we saw the sunset and knew the old had passed once again. The next day we began our search for the 9-5 jobs our family longed for during that season.

Being born into a family full of women and hard workers created a work ethic that pours through my veins. You could say we are borderline workaholics. Also marrying into a family with those same values, it became no surprise that I dove into the insurance industry the way I did. I landed a job with a mentor who taught me everything he knew. He saw something in me, and I longed to be the best for him and myself.

On my second day, I was still finding my way into this new position when I was jolted into a passion that changed it all. My husband picked me up for lunch on that overcast and snowy day. One minute I was going on and on about what I was learning and the next we were spinning out of control getting on the highway. Our vehicle finally stopped and we thought, "What just happened?" At that moment, we believed we had escaped a terrible accident until we looked out the passenger window and saw a van coming directly at my side. Everything flashed and we braced for the impact. By the grace of God, I was cut out of the vehicle and checked at the hospital for only minor injuries. Getting home, we rested and started dealing with the insurance. Six months prior I had called to get a policy and they never asked a single question. The real nightmare began that moment realizing I did not have proper protection. Such fear came over me with the idea of possibly losing everything we had worked so hard for. Through this accident, a passion was born for people and protection that is hard to match even to this day. This new role would become where I made my mark and fulfilled my dreams. Not just dreams of caring for and providing for my family, but dreams of making a difference, building significance, and spreading my voice. That may sound ridiculous, but I believe in the importance of what insurance protects and how not having insurance can impact your life.

Those first few years, I was a sponge soaking up everything insurance. Every morning I stuck to a solid routine, dressed with purpose, and went into the office to push myself. My daily mission became making sure each person I came in contact with left better than they came. Whether that was just knowledge or with a new policy and an agent to lean on. This long stage of life became the season of learning I was good at something on my own.

It's now twenty years, four states, and two businesses later. I currently have my own insurance agency and started a social media management company. I went from fleeing my past in New Jersey to chasing my dreams. Has it been easy or fallen into my lap? Hell no! Many pivots, days of analyzing, tears, sleepless nights, and praying to God for success occurred.

You see, when I began my insurance agency, I followed the directions given to me such as, "hire a ton of employees" and "buy leads, you've got to spend money to make money." I found myself spending my way to a slow death in my pursuit of financial success and freedom. I began losing faith in my dreams and more importantly myself with each day, I felt myself slipping back into that girl that boarded a plane at 17 years old…lost, afraid, and letting others dictate what my business and life should look like. I had come so far, yet still faced with the same battles. The difference this time was I knew in my soul I could trust my instincts and follow what I had done before to make significant changes that were more aligned with the business I envisioned. I was the one in control, the answers and the ability were all within me.

The shift came one early Saturday morning as I was alone in my office. It always starts with getting alone with myself. I'm not sure if that is due to being an only child or if that is just how I'm wired. Walking into my office that morning, the first thing I noticed was the sun beaming through the windows beating an acknowledgement into me that a new day had come. There wasn't another soul in sight and I found myself dancing and soaking in the realization of my surroundings and what I had built up to that point. I had made a lot of mistakes and followed a path that needed repaving, but it was my path to repave and I knew I had the knowledge, tools, and determination to do it. I spent the next 12 hours with the music blasting while facing the reality of my business head-on. I poured into spreadsheets and processes, tracked all numbers, and devoured my bank statements.

I made huge strides and realizations that day, with the biggest being a humble understanding that I needed help, not the kind of help I had been given reassuring me that I can buy my way into success. As much as I had learned and experienced, it was still not enough for me to have a vision of what was needed. The road I was on was a lonely one like many other business owners. They don't tell you about the uncertainty, lows, or self-doubt that weaves its way into the day-to-day operations. I was clear on what I wanted, but being so close to the situation emotionally, I couldn't form the path on my own.

The answers to my prayers were answered when I remembered where and how I started years ago - with a mentor. I immediately sought out a mentor in my industry again. Finding Cassidy shifted everything for me. She is a business coach who specializes in female insurance agents. Not only did Cassidy understand the industry, but she had built her business and life the exact way I had dreamt about for my own. Her action steps and belief in me pushed me to make the changes I needed to make immediately starting on day one. At this point, I had read all the books and attained the carnal understanding required, but her program gave me the confidence and path I needed. I was no longer on an island fishing for my next meal, I had the full course at my fingertips with an ally beside me.

The steps were simple but not always easy. I went from spending thousands a month on leads and marketing with 6 employees down to zero spend and 2 employees. I was scared out of my mind, this was the complete opposite of what I had been told and how I had been operating. Being the risk taker and doer that I am, I dove in with courage, but shaking in fear. I listened and implemented every single thing I was told to do, placing trust in myself and Cassidy. The faith that I had in us paid off within 90 days. I was doing more with so much less. I had streamlined processes and I had also begun working with Ati, a branding coach. I was no longer buying and chasing leads, I was now attracting them as business was coming to me.

Looking back on that Saturday morning when I danced alone in my office feeling proud of where I was even while knowing change had to come, still brings a smile to my face over two years later. That day was an ending and a beginning like many other peaks and valleys in my life. The path is paved for the pivot through the same three things - acknowledgement, contemplation, and resilience. Through every shift, my confidence multiplied. I have since slashed my overhead even further by going completely virtual. I still run my insurance agency with only 2 employees and each day I wake up to messages from prospects instead of swiping my credit card for a lead. The philosophy of spending more will never be my truth again.

Without shining light on my situation and desires that sunny day, I never would have known what was still to come. Up until that moment, I believed I was on a one-way path with only some twists and turns. Little did I know that it contained forks and intersections. A new door and passion that I never imagined appeared. This quiet introvert found a place in the social media marketing world because she needed to stop spending. Like insurance, I proved myself good at something that I could share with the world.

Today, you can find me mixing the two passions together. My life changed on a flight at 17 years old and helped me develop the skills I needed for each transformation since. I have lived in 9 states now, been involved in multiple businesses, and still dance before work in my home office. I believe we can all change our path in a matter of a few minutes or one flight across the country. Looking within, acknowledging, contemplating and resilience is all that is needed.

Where do you find yourself today? Before I boarded that plane I was so defeated and could only focus on the mistakes and helplessness in my heart. Sitting with my truth without distractions or other voices revealed a deeper story. If your starting point is one of despair and uncertainty begin asking yourself the following questions:

1. What is the TRUTH of the current situation? These are not assumptions or perceptions, only the truth of the matter.

    a. Who am I listening to for advice? Are they to be trusted?
    b. In what small way can I change the story today?
    c. Who do I need to forgive (yourself included)?
    d. How long have I been living in this current state?

2. How did I get here? At what step did things start feeling wrong?

    a. Did I involve new people along the way?
    b. Did I neglect relationships that you should have nourished? If so, who and why?
    c. Did I start thinking I had it all together and didn't need others?
    d. Have I been forcing my way and relying only on myself because I didn't want to hear that I was wrong or face not getting my own way?
    e. Do I truly want what I'm trying to accomplish or am I living a life that someone else told me to live?

If you are anything like me, you might not like the answers to some of these questions. It may hit home and try to create a sense of self-loathing. Do not let that creep in. Keep going - this is just one step and often a short one. You must know how you got to this point in order to change and develop the strength to see yourself in your own story in a truthful light. This is not a time to devour yourself, just a quick glimpse into your part of the story. Give grace to yourself and know that this is the path to freedom.

Now that you have an idea of where you are actually at, it is time to outline the new plot. Answer the following questions.

1. What makes me unique?
2. What drives me and brings joy into my life?
3. What do others love about me?
4. Who do I turn to when I need encouragement? What could I do to encourage myself?
5. What do I do better than everyone I know?
6. What are 3 things I've done in my life that I'm proud of? This can be anything big or small.
7. What has helped me in the past when I felt defeated or ready for a change?
8. Who do I know that is living the way I want to live? What qualities do they have?

All of these questions will illustrate the reason you are at this moment and serve as a reminder of where you want to be. It is true what they say, you are the author of your life and story. You choose your path and the mark you want to leave behind…which is your brand. You got into business because you want to make a difference and you had the guts to take the first step. Don't quit now just because you may not see the next step. The next moves will reveal the map. You never need all the answers, only trust in yourself and your abilities. Let's start paving the path.

1. Do I need to remove anyone currently around me? Remember, I went from 6 to 2 employees - you might need to do the same.
2. What are 3 core values that are non-negotiables for me?
3. Does everyone around me adhere to those same core values? If not, they need to be removed, especially from your business.

4. Who pours into me and my business that I'm not paying? Book a coffee, lunch, or call with them. Tell them you are grateful for their part in your life.

If you do not have anyone currently, find someone that you can be that for. The door will open for you to have someone who does the same for you. More importantly, it will form the ability to be that for yourself.

1. Who can I hire, follow online, or reach out to in my industry that can help me elevate to the vision I had when I started?
2. Do I need some training in certain areas of my business?
3. Are there areas I can delegate or outsource to make things more productive and joyful?

I know I'm not alone in this, but one of the biggest areas I had to work through was admitting I wasn't good at certain things. Growing up I never felt like I could make a mistake or fail. I was willing to sacrifice my own well-being for approval. As I got older, I had this idea that I needed to be perfect at all things within my life and business while appearing as if I loved doing it at the same time. Free yourself today from the notion that you need to be everything, and love all things within your business. When I stopped to think on a deeper level about myself and my business, I realized quickly that I was not showing up authentically. I was relying on others to write my story. I never went into business to follow an instruction manual. I wanted freedom with a voice to make a difference and do things my way. I'm sure you are the same way. You might be thinking that it is just wishful thinking or you have learned that isn't how it truly is. I would say, find that spark you had when you started again but now add in the wisdom you have gained. You can have both without despair.

This is not meant to be an exhaustive list of what needs to go into the changes you may need to make but one thing is certain - it starts with a truthful look at yourself, your situation, and an idea of what you are truly wanting. Those first steps will give you a beginning point of reference. One step is all it takes.

You have gotten this far, now you need to bring it all together. Go look at yourself in the mirror, really look at yourself, and tell yourself the truth. You are where you are right now, but the story is changing. Recognizing the truth and your part along with a determination to take action will transform your tomorrows.

Actions and truths I live by:

Get real with yourself. Who you are, where you have been, and where you want to go.

Admit mistakes, forgive yourself, and offer forgiveness to others.

Understand that life not only comes with twists and turns but also crossroads.

Get help along the way. Life is meant to be shared. Connect with people who are aligned with you and honor yourself by removing people who aren't.

Never be afraid to start again or change. Some people will never understand or agree but that is their issue to work through, not yours!

When you hurt someone, own it and grow through it. I have hurt people that I love dearly, but choosing to take accountability has never been a mistake.

If you don't like where you are, STOP, THINK, and SHIFT what you are doing. Take inventory and take the steps necessary to change it. Whatever you do, don't keep living a life you don't love.

Growth only comes from honesty with yourself, others, and your situation.

Once you know yourself and your desires, you can share with others. This is the door that opens up the miracles of life. You will take your business to new heights and your life to an altitude that others long for. You don't need to move across the country, leave your current life behind, or find yourself completely alone starting over. If you are alone or feel alone, it is still possible. You have everything you need within yourself to not only change your world but the world around you as well.

Remember that what you want for yourself is also needed in the world for others. Seek the help you may need along the way. You might also need a new view with a different landscape, but it is all possible when you map it out for yourself through truth, wisdom, and action.

In closing, I dare you to dance in the sun with pride, reminding yourself where you are and what you have accomplished. Sit down and get real with yourself. Look at your surroundings and take note of things you want to change and keep. Find people who will dance with you, speak truth to your situation, and offer to be part of the transition you are just beginning. Take the time to write out the vision you see when you think about a life you not only want but already started. You are not stuck and more than likely you are only one 5-hour flight away from the life you dream of.

Angelle Sanders

AF Career Marketing
Career Coach & Resume Writer

www.linkedin.com/company/af-career-marketing-strategies
https://www.facebook.com/angelle.sanders/
https://www.instagram.com/angelle_ferrer/
https://afcareermarketing.com/

Angelle shines as a source of inspiration in the worlds of Career Coaching and Content Writing, having appeared on popular platforms like the Be You Brand podcast and Opting-Out to Start Up show. When the pandemic prompted a shift in her why, she embraced career coaching in 2022 with a mission to empower others.

With over 17 years of experience in IT, business, and product management, Angelle knows the obstacles that can hold us back – from barriers and misconceptions to limiting labels. Instead of letting these challenges deter her, she forged ahead, creating a roadmap to success that now guides others on their journey.

Driven by a desire to help professionals thrive in today's ever-changing job market, Angelle now focuses on supporting individuals facing career transition. Outside of work, she finds joy in adventures with her loved ones, cherishing each moment of shared growth and discovery.

For those seeking guidance and encouragement to reach their full potential, Angelle offers a path forward. Explore her transformative insights and personalized support at www.afcareermarketing.com, and begin your journey of self-discovery and empowerment today.

Discovery in Pieces

By Angelle Sanders

I am not a puzzle person. My daughter is, and during Covid, this was one of our "pandemic hobbies." Puzzles are an interesting activity that requires patience, time, and focus. I enjoy them, but it's really something I enjoy doing with someone. What I found interesting was how people have different approaches to working through a puzzle. For example, my daughter likes to start with the end pieces to build the outer frame. I like to begin by sorting pieces by color and pattern. As we build out the outer frame and patterns stand out, I can quickly dig for matching pieces. I favor efficiency and do not want to spend an hour looking through pieces that don't matter. They're a distraction, hiding the gems waiting to be discovered.

Over the months of working through multiple 1,500-piece puzzles, my daughter and I celebrated as we found those impossible-to-find pieces. We experienced joy as we completed entire sections of a difficult puzzle, and the sense of accomplishment when those sections came together to complete an entire corner of the puzzle. Slowly each picture would come into view.

Another observation was how each person has patience in different aspects of the process. My daughter enjoys solving sections with more plain pieces that have little patterns, where you're forced to figure out how each piece fits one by one. Imagine going through individual pieces and rotating each until you find a match. Since my eyes gravitate to patterns, building out patterns becomes my quest. As puzzle teams go, we actually make a complimentary team!

Regardless of the puzzle style, as we reach the final section, you can't help the sense of focus and excitement that begins to build. This is it! Our goal is near! The finish line is just around the corner. I recall one puzzle as we approached those final pieces, we reached the end to discover a final piece was missing. It was devastating, to say the least. All of the time, work, and dedication, knowing the final picture would never be complete. As human beings, we're motivated to work towards completing a picture. Being robbed of this victory, or closure, was a bummer.

I heard a mentor once say, "We are never still in life. We are always growing towards something or away from something else." Puzzles provide a great lesson in discovering our identity and who we are meant to be. They illustrate how every small step in our journey is an essential piece to a larger picture. Even the smallest pieces matter. Each has a unique role to play and is crucial for the whole to be realized.

Each of us has unique skills, experiences, passions, and perspectives that make us who we are, which only expand and evolve as we grow. Yet, how often do we undersell ourselves, ignoring and/or neglecting the most impactful parts of who we are? We cannot take a single piece for granted because just as a puzzle remains incomplete without all its pieces, our identity, and purpose will feel incomplete when experiences, insights, and personal qualities are missing. Overlooking them is robbing yourself of a victory that is to come. Our power becomes the culmination of everything we've experienced and developed throughout our lives, which fuels our passions, hopes, dreams, and goals as the next pieces to our puzzles.

Youth

Looking back, I recognize puzzle pieces I completely missed from my youth, particularly around the circumstances and experiences in my upbringing. Growing up in the military is a significant part of who I am, though growing up it often felt like the source of many setbacks as I got older. The experience of frequently moving and starting new schools. Feeling forever the new girl. Each new beginning meant starting over, feeling alone, and having to make friends all over again. Unfortunately, kids are not always kind to the socially awkward new girl in school. The worst was when teachers brought me to the front of the class on the first day of a new school to be introduced. I was already shy, just put me out of my misery! I made friends here and there, but I learned to keep to myself early on. Part of my identity growing up was knowing peers generally did not accept me. This was a limiting belief that stuck and would take years to discover the true value of this part of my story.

Which began to unfold at age 17. After years of frequent knee injuries, I went to see a specialist, a few x-rays, and an MRI later, I was told to start working out and strengthen the muscles around my knees. If not, our next discussion would be a knee replacement. I was overall healthy; my kneecap just wouldn't stay in place. In my young mind, "Did he just say surgery and knee replacement in the same sentence?" That was enough to shock me into action. I signed up for my first gym membership that same week. Part of it was fear of a potential surgery and what the recovery would mean, the other part was a determination to prove him wrong. As I ventured into the world of fitness, I discovered something unexpected. It turned out I LOVE this stuff! Strength training and especially boot camp-style HIIT workouts. Biking, jogging, and hiking. Cardio kickboxing, where do I sign up? Yes, I enjoyed the toning effect on my body and how it made me feel. What I truly enjoyed were workouts that made me feel strong. At some point, I caught myself beginning to tell people it was my inner Army girl coming out.

I also developed a sense of adventure. That happens when you have lived overseas and have visited nearly every castle across West Germany. Old military bunkers, underground salt caves, historic sites, along with a short trip to Paris all by age 11. This resulted in a wish list that included destinations around the world and adventures such as skydiving, hiking up a volcano, camping in the Grand Canyon, and even getting a tattoo. Skydiving itself was never a top dream, however my father was a paratrooper in the Army. It terrified me, but in my mind, if anyone was going to do this, it would be a paratrooper's kid right? I also learned that the best way to overcome a fear was to go straight through it, knees trembling and all. At age 17, the boldness that began to grow and mix with the awkward shyness did not want to accept I would wimp out.

I additionally discovered my view of "family" differed from most. Growing up in the military, you do not get to grow up around relatives and cousins. You travel with your immediate family only. Everyone arrives at a military base among strangers. It's your parents' unit that becomes your family. They are with whom you spend holidays and birthdays and go through life with. Simply put, I grew up knowing that family was more than blood. In addition, I came from a large Hispanic family that was loud, committed, and always together. Friends I would meet as a teenager would not understand this dedication about me. I was committed to them like family, included them in family events, and hoped for the same. For my close friends, I simply knew no other way. Some would interpret this as "clingy" or weak-minded, and many would take advantage of my deep commitment. It also meant I was often disappointed when people did not reciprocate. As a young person, I took it personally for the longest time before I came to this realization about myself. After this, I began to recognize it as a view from my unique upbringing. I decided I liked my view more and over time, sought to overlook what others simply couldn't understand. In time, this turned from an insecurity and I recognized it as a strength.

Another gift I've only begun to unpack in recent years is a resilience I did not know was there. I cannot count how many schools I attended growing up. My high school years alone included four high schools across three different states. Military families become experts at packing and unpacking a home, and my family had it down to an art. I'm discovering that constant change and adapting have equipped me to work through change and the "unexpected" as an adult. I see many who struggle with this. There is fear of change, so many hesitate and avoid it. Life will bring change, but every day we continue to breathe and grow, change becomes for our good. A tragedy in life is one that does not change or evolve. Change can often be long and difficult, but my upbringing taught me to be more fluid with change and find ways to roll with it rather than resist it. I recognize that no matter how often my surroundings changed, the constant was my family. My parents and brother. As long as they were there, I was home. This made everything changing around me easier to accept because I had the rock I leaned on.

I now know that resilience, adaptability, adventure, strength, and a strong sense of family are the most precious gifts from my childhood. If I had remained stuck on the rejection and insecurities from my youth, I would have never been open to discovering and choosing to step into these parts of my identity.

If you were to see my puzzle, these would be foundational end pieces that hold the rest of who I am with strength and security.

What core values, strengths, and experiences from your childhood years have become foundational to who you are today? Experiences can be good or bad, but we overcome, learn, and grow from them all. Add them to your puzzle.

Post College

Experiences that hurt or shatter our confidence will come in life. For me, one such experience was during my first career opportunity after college. I was never short of ambition and drive, and I was beginning a career in technology. To say it can be a high-pressure work environment is an understatement of the century. This first work experience was also where I faced my first hostile work environment. After a couple of years, I was promoted to one of two team leads. My role was to ensure the quality of client deliveries, foster collaboration, solve problems, and support my team. We thought we were leading well. No one had told us otherwise.

I do not know what led this manager to do this, but I will state up front this company was known for high employee turnover and bad management. They expected heavy overtime to meet deadlines and as a young mother, I often worked until midnight. I recall a meeting with my manager, who informed me that my performance did not meet expectations. I was placed on an "observation" period with a list of areas to improve. There would also be weekly check-ins. I recall a couple of items on this list seemed superficial, but I put my best foot forward regardless to prove my worth. I had two babies in diapers at this point and could not afford to lose my job, especially after everything I had accomplished up to this point. By week two, this manager acknowledged some improvements but focused on recording any little missteps. By week three, continued scrutiny over every little decision. I was filled with frustration and a growing fear. Afraid of making a mistake, I began to doubt myself and my capabilities and questioned everything. I also began to consider that I would be unable to meet her unclear expectations. By week four it became clear. For whatever reason, I was being pushed out. It did not matter what I did; this manager was determined to discredit me in order to legally justify letting me go. This turned into a hellish month going to work every day with a sense of fear, criticism, and doubt, all telling me I was not enough. I went over the events with trusted counsel hoping to discover what I possibly did to deserve this mistreatment, and the consensus was that this manager was likely struggling in her own job and looking for people to blame.

I left this company with my confidence shattered and a healthy list of limiting beliefs about myself. After all, this was my first career opportunity out of college! I decided to take some time and comb through my years at this company. I noted all of the "firsts"— achievements, my first career promotion, recognitions, special projects—and what I volunteered for above and beyond. Leading new hire training, successful client deliveries, coaching team members, and other quality measures. I would like to say that I knew this was the smart thing to do, but deep down I needed to prove to myself that I was worth more than how I was treated. This was the best decision!

Part of overcoming the limiting beliefs that aim to hold us back is to first acknowledge them. Then reflect and challenge the narrative. Look at what the facts from the successes and achievements tell you. Sure, we always have opportunities for growth, but silence the negative voices and allow the good to speak. Replace the negative thoughts with truth to come out with more empowering thoughts. Confiding in trusted counsel was another step to overcoming limiting beliefs since it's easy to have blinders about ourselves. Notice I do not say friends or family here because not everyone is comfortable being candid or can give constructive wisdom. By the time I began interviews for my next career opportunity, the steps I had taken to rebuild my confidence helped me avoid getting stuck in the emotions of it. During this process, I laid down the foundation I would build the next step of my career upon. I came out on the other side seeing the growth and strength that came from that situation with integrity.

In the end, I discovered new foundational pieces to my puzzle: self-awareness, emotional intelligence, decision-making, communication, humility, coaching, collaboration, teamwork, conflict resolution, and integrity.

What are the foundational pieces to your puzzle you have collected through different trials? Have you slowed down to acknowledge them? Add them to your puzzle.

Mid-Career

We often find limiting beliefs are imposed on us just as we can impose them on ourselves. There is no shortage of standards and beliefs pressed onto us in today's culture from our family, media, society, and professional environments. We call them limiting beliefs because they have the power to hold us back if we believe them. It's also worth noting this can be something we consciously or subconsciously choose to believe. Remember, we are never completely still in life. We are always moving towards something or away from something else, and ultimately this is up to us.

When we accept or allow a limiting belief, this can affect us in many ways. Doubt, insecurities, fear, depression, and hesitation can creep in causing us to emotionally and/or physically hide, give up, or worse, never try. Each of these moves us away from potential opportunities. Away from possibility. A difficult place where I faced imposed limiting beliefs has been in the workplace, in the form of workplace biases. Not just with those extreme type-A personalities, but gender bias and biases that can come from different divisions or departments within a company. By now, I've worked with type-A men and women, and I no longer shy away from these situations having experienced the strong partners they can become. Other forms of bias are more challenging to overcome.

A more subtle bias I've discovered is often felt by someone looking to cross career boundaries or change careers. I experienced this at multiple points having started out in technology, moved to business, and then later crossed into product. Each move took over a year of preparation, as it should because changing careers is a more difficult job change situation. I was good at researching job descriptions and making plans to fill skill gaps while building exposure and experience. The first time I heard that I was "too tech" and not enough "business," my initial response was to prove myself more. Later when I heard I was too "business" and not enough "product," I began to notice a pattern.

These comments typically came from individuals in the area where I was trying to go. Yes, we need to prove we can do the job, this is part of marketing ourselves. However, what's become clear is there's another side to this bias in how individuals view those with different backgrounds. I can share accomplishments and success stories that show I am qualified. I can pursue additional training, but if they have concluded I am simply to be the "technology person" and are unwilling to see me any different, they're less likely to give me a chance. This is an example of someone imposing limiting beliefs and assumptions on what I can or cannot do before I'm even given the chance to prove otherwise. Concluding how I think or the limits of my thinking, because of my background, that I'm "too tech" to have a "business mind," is a mistake. Many are extremely product and customer-centric, with technology minds.

After getting the job, I would continue to be overlooked for special projects when new managers came in with initial assumptions until we worked more closely together, even after I was well-established with my team for over five years. One very frustrating year, I leaned heavily on my unique background because at that point they needed someone who could lead production issues, speak tech, and jump in to fill a gap. Enter Angelle stage right! Up to this point, a part of me had kept trying to be "more this" or "more that" to fit what I thought this manager was looking for. I had a year where I lost all drive and ambition and I did the bare minimum. I mentally "checked out." I experienced a year of feeling defeated, because what's the point? It led to a form of depression because I was always involved in something. This went against my above-and-beyond work ethic, which only confirmed the down state I was in, which deepened the depression. During this time, however, what they needed was exactly what I had. I saw the need and sprung into action, which livened me! This season brought the AHA moment. I finally saw how my background and experience up to this point, along with every transferrable skill, came together. I looked around and saw that not many peers would have been able to successfully navigate this for our team. I realized I had a unique value proposition. This brought me out of my funk and after this, I stopped worrying about what I lacked, continued to focus on growth, and began to develop a confidence that gave me the courage to stop sitting around and get active in my career growth once again.

Consider the puzzle pieces I developed while I went through these situations: marketing myself, goal setting, learning agility, adaptability, communication, presenting my value, networking, self-assessment, and career planning. Even allowing myself to step back and process the emotions I needed to deal with took courage. Plus, after multiple successful moves, I also had a well-rounded perspective across technology, business, and product which are now a key part of my story. All of this now heavily influences a unique perspective.

When has someone imposed a limiting belief or restriction you refused to believe? Think of the steps you took to overcome it. What is now part of your story and puzzle because you did not give up? Add this to your puzzle.

Finding Passion

As we navigate through life's seasons, it's easy to become self-focused while we figure out life. Inevitably, we hit tough periods when we're focused on simply trying to survive, and it's easy to get stuck in survival mode. I recall reaching a point where I was tired of merely getting by. I wanted to know what it was like to THRIVE. I even remember the feeling of one day declaring out loud—"I am done just surviving, I want to thrive!" This declaration felt good, even though I had no idea what it meant to thrive. It never crossed my mind to ask someone, everyone I knew seemed to be in survival mode as well. I didn't think to even Google it. In prayer and meditation what my heart clung to was one simple truth: to thrive meant "beyond me." It meant living in a way that I could impact and uplift those around me—not just within my four walls with my family and children. The ability to impact outward, not simply inward.

This idea was a gift and it started small. I began to take action where I could. During COVID, there was a great need for service, with food pantries, at our church, to opening my home up as a micro-school for children I knew. This ended up with 4 children in total who were struggling at home alone during this most difficult time. It was exhausting, but it was a labor of love. Setting up multiple workstations across my home, six feet apart, disinfecting each surface, door handle, and chair every morning. One of the children had asthma, so we had designated "mask off" areas for class time and tape marking six feet for her safety. My breaks from working at home were spent ensuring everyone was logged on and there were no internet issues or troubles with online learning, which were frequent. The gift was so these kids could still socialize and not feel alone and isolated. It also gave me the opportunity to see those moments when they were frustrated, holding back tears, ready to give up, and/or ready to stop trying. It reached a point I could just tell by simply walking into the room and seeing the expression on their faces. In these moments, everything stopped and it was all about that child.

The truth is the more I focused outward, the more peace I experienced inward. It also brought a sense of fulfillment and empowerment; empowering because I learned I did not need to make a big impact to make a difference where I already was. It also helped me take control of my own thoughts. When focusing inward, my mind becomes easily cluttered with my own wants, dreams, struggles, insecurities, and self-imposed busyness. Seeing life through a different set of lenses, I was able to acknowledge but not be consumed by "me." It did not mean I did anything at the expense of my responsibilities, family, or well-being. It was an imperfect balance I needed to learn.

Embracing my heart for others gave me a profound sense of purpose. The word "embrace" means to "include or integrate something as part of a whole, recognizing its value and incorporating it fully." When I chose to integrate this heart for others into my life, I chose to let it become a driving passion in my mind and heart.

I like to think this added to my puzzle: thrive, service, passion, sacrifice, purpose, and fulfillment. Although, as a mother, a few of those were already there, but now with added depth.

Have you experienced a moment where you discovered a passion? What new corner of your puzzle did this illuminate in your life? A new corner to now explore? Add it to your puzzle.

Entrepreneur

Too many stepping stones led to 2022 when I embraced a crazy notion that I was made for "more." I was made for a purpose. I began to pursue credentials as a career coach and resume writer to help women and those in business, technology, and product. What triggered this interest you might ask? I had always been considered a "high achiever" at work. I'm driven and find fulfillment in going the extra mile. I'm also a bit of a nerd—I love discovering gaps or inefficiencies and researching, planning, and implementing improvements. Even when technology-related, I am excited to research usability, data flow, and system processes to envision enhancements and see them come to life.

I came to the conclusion I would always have this drive to achieve and be involved in something, and that I could either dedicate my "above and beyond" to boosting a company's bottom line or choose to use it to build something that empowers others. I was already the go-to writing resumes for family and friends since college, already a mentor and coach, so it seemed like a natural fit.

This transition surfaced overwhelmingly limiting beliefs in myself. Insecurities, self-doubt, and fear like I never experienced before. I felt insecure about marketing, even talking about this on social media, and sharing offers with my network. I recall being so scared to post my first offer and those first consultation calls with people on the phone. I did not feel credible. I came from a comfortable position in a career of leading, where I could do my job well half asleep. There was a confidence in this. This move took me back to entry-level, feeling like I knew nothing. I doubted my writing and presentation skills despite having done both for decades with business-level and technical documents. Self-doubt ran through my mind like, "Who would listen to me?" and "What if I can't help them?" plagued me. I was in a new world, out of my element and comfort zone, stretched like never before

This journey has also been the steepest learning curve I've ever faced—Mount Everest steep. I got really good at ramping up on a new project. Quickly caught up and learned everything I needed to so that I could jump in quickly and add value. Meeting those farther along in the same industry also triggered the worst case of imposter syndrome. It often caused me to shut down. Many hard lessons were learned these past two years, about learning to pace myself, not try to grow too quickly. Timeboxing my schedule for my family and giving myself the grace to take a break and enjoy the journey have been the important lessons I needed to learn.

I have also needed to remind myself of my "why" every step of the way. Remember it's not about recognition or followers or speaking events. It's about building something that empowers others and can change the direction of clients' lives and their families. One person at a time, just as my journey has evolved one step at a time.

This new chapter in my life has illuminated a larger corner of my puzzle because it has illuminated possibilities I would have never known if I had not taken the steps. Revealing skills and strengths I did not know I had.

The new pieces I can proudly add to my puzzle: courage, confidence, boldness, marketing, writing, sales, speech, a deepened understanding of faith, trust, patience, discipline, strategy, collaboration, creativity, solving problems, coaching, and mentoring.

Has life led to discovering a new dream? What has developed since you took that step and every step since? What new lessons and skills have you developed and discovered in yourself? How have you grown as a result? Add these to your puzzle.

Embrace the Journey—Every Experience Counts

In this journey, victories come in many forms. Larger victories are really the outcome of each small victory leading up to it. The beauty of this journey is that with each victory, we learn more about ourselves. Remember my daughter in our puzzle story, that she was the one to go through and check every piece? Rotate it; if it doesn't fit, grab the next and try again. Each small victory is like finding that small piece that fits perfectly in place, bringing you one step closer to a more complete picture of who you are.

A mentor during college gave a piece of advice I follow to this day: "If you've done it once, that's experience. Write that down." Let's ponder this for a moment. If you have tried something new in your personal life, at work, whether you wanted to or not. That's experience; write that down. If you volunteered at a charity that took you out of your comfort zone. That's experience; write that down. I apply this approach when working with women to discover their transferrable skills and value propositions. If we cannot see the value we truly offer, how can we market ourselves effectively? I have not worked with one woman who was not missing one or more skills. Some skills we simply cannot see in ourselves and other skills we do not recognize as valuable!

This concept applies just as much to myself in this current season. Embrace the journey because every experience counts. Each challenge, triumph, and setback is just as vital to your puzzle. Together, they form a unique and powerful picture of who you are. These pieces fill in the smaller gaps that can complete entire aspects of who we are and who we are growing into!

Picture you have a mason jar to fill with rocks and sand. The rocks are the fundamental parts of your identity, and the sand is the smaller experiences and victories across your life. Imagine trying to fill your jar with the sand first and rocks on top—the rocks would never fit. Now put in your rocks, or fundamental aspects of your identity first, and then let the sand fill in the gaps. We will always accomplish more when we are leveraging the whole of who we are.

When was the last time you slowed to reflect on new experiences and skills from the past 12 months to 3 years? What are you overlooking that is the sand to your jar?

Glimpses into Your Big Picture

We all have those AHA moments—those flashes of insight where the pieces of our life's puzzle begin to come together and reveal a bigger purpose. These are most often the result of moving forward, taking steps, and working through failures. These moments can reveal unexpected paths and opportunities that align with our natural gifts and passions, guiding us toward our true purpose. These moments will look different for each of us.

One such moment for me came when I realized a calling to work with professionals to advance their careers through career coaching and resume writing. This was not something I ever considered, wanted, or ever planned to do. It was a realization that came at a faith-based entrepreneur event. An amazing speaker reminded us that business ideas do not have to be big or glamorous. Some of the best business ideas are most often simple and serve a need. The audience was then challenged to think through what we were naturally good at, our natural gifts. He asked us to think of areas we already help others with using these natural gifts. In that moment the thought came to mind of working with family and friends on their resumes and job search over the years, because jobs are a practical need. Yes, the process can be tedious, but with perspective, it can be simplified and made less complicated.

If like me you believe things happen for a reason, then you'll love this. Just before sitting down to hear this speaker at this event, I had just met a single mom during lunch who was worried about the economy. She needed a better-paying job because she was constantly overworked and her company would not offer a raise or opportunities for advancement. She was worried about how she would put food on the table for her son if something did not change. Just 20 minutes before this speaker would begin offering wisdom and challenging thoughts from his super successful business, I had just offered to help her update her resume to help simplify the complicated. The moment the idea hit, imagine the light bulb as bright as a spotlight shining down on me where I sat.

This AHA moment would have never occurred if I had not taken the step to buy a ticket to my first entrepreneur event EVER. I would have never bought the ticket if I had not done other side gigs in the past while working in a career I did enjoy, which at some point led to a desire that if I was going to spend my life doing something, I wanted to spend it doing something that mattered.

These moments of clarity—whether they lead to starting a business, changing careers, or discovering a new passion—are glimpses of uncovering our true purpose. These moments are building the big picture of our lives. As we reflect on these moments and the AHA moments they bring, we come to understand and appreciate the unique journey that has shaped who we are today.

When you reflect on your journey, where are the AHA moments that uncovered a new path or affirmed an existing one? What chance or step of faith did you need to take that led to clarity?

Keep It Simple

Notice that each of my stories started with a limiting belief, except for the AHA moment. The truth is our emotions can blind us and we need to work through these limiting beliefs to discover what's on the other side. The resistance, moments of doubt, and limiting beliefs will try to hold us back and cause us to feel stuck. Their goal is to send us right back to surviving, never to thrive. A simple strategy to counteract these lies is to combat them with truth. This doesn't happen overnight, but it does allow us to build ourselves up to move beyond the moment. Our goal is the next time a situation triggers that negative belief, we are armed with a response. Saying it to yourself will feel fake at first, because you may not truly believe it in yourself. Yet. As confidence and faith build, in time we move past these moments more quickly. That's how you know you're progressing!

We also discover that on the other side of each limiting belief is a missing piece to the bigger picture of who we are.

Too many stepping stones led to the pivotal moment and decision to step into the entrepreneurial world. I would have never reached this moment if I had not been open to discovery and challenging my limiting beliefs along the way. It can be a limiting belief holding you back in relationships, discovering your passion, entering the next stage in life, or in your health.

Whatever it is my hope is you can apply these basic steps and join me in the journey towards discovering the big picture to our life's puzzles. Life will be hard, but there is fulfillment and joy when we are doing what we are uniquely created for.

Five Steps to Overcoming a Limiting Belief:

- **Identify and Acknowledge:** Recognize and admit you have a limiting belief about yourself. A simple truth: It's difficult to resist something we refuse to admit is even there.

- **Challenge and Reframe:** Question what the belief is telling you. Replace it with more positive, empowering thoughts. If you struggle here, share with someone you trust who knows you. Allow others to empower you.

- **Positive Affirmations:** Use affirmations to reinforce a positive self-image and your potential. Another approach is to replace the lies with truth.

- **Seek Support:** These can be mentors, coaches, or therapists who can provide guidance and support. Peers who have overcome similar situations are also great because they have already walked this path and succeeded.

- **Take Action:** Start with small steps to build confidence and prove the beliefs wrong. You do this through new experiences and successes. Consider a snowball when it rolls down a hill. Start small and let the momentum build.

Experiences and lessons in life can be illuminating in unexpected ways. Every experience, challenge, and triumph adds to the intricate puzzle of who we are. Like the pieces my daughter and I meticulously placed during our pandemic puzzle sessions, each moment of growth and discovery contributes to a clearer picture.

As I continue to uncover each new lesson in life, I see a bigger picture coming into view. Remember, the journey isn't just about the end goal but about cherishing every step along the way.

So, keep going through, not around, and celebrate every piece you find that brings you closer to the complete picture of who you are meant to be.

Cat Coley

Cat Coley, Bounce Back L.A.B.
Storytelling Coach, Keynote Speaker & Podcast Host

https://www.linkedin.com/in/therealcatcoley/
https://www.facebook.com/therealcatcoley
https://www.instagram.com/therealcatcoley/
https://catcoley.com/

Cat Coley, a powerhouse of inspiration who turned her lowest point into a launchpad for a life-changing calling as a storytelling coach, keynote speaker, published author, podcast host and soon-to-be magazine columnist.

Cat's past is not just a story she tells; it's the foundation of her mission to empower women entrepreneurs & creatives to embrace their own stories.

When Cat speaks, people listen —captivated by her authenticity and moved by her courage to share what most keep hidden. As one event host noted, Hearing Cat's story changes you. She's more than a speaker; she's a spark for change. Once you hear her story, you'll always remember it.

With Cat, you're not just learning how to tell your story; you're learning how to live boldly and inspire others by simply owning your story and being your true self.

Unscripted: Finding Beauty in the Mess

By Cat Coley

Life rarely sticks to the script. If mine were a movie, it'd definitely be one of those quirky indie films where you leave the theater thinking, "Well, that was…unexpected." But here's the thing about offbeat movies and offbeat lives: they leave a mark. They're memorable, not in spite of their twists and turns, but because of them. So welcome to my journey, my very own indie film aptly titled "Finding Beauty in the Mess."

The Plot Twist Nobody Asked For

Have you ever had an out-of-body experience? No, not the alien-abducted kind (although that would be quite a story), but the feeling that you're watching yourself from above? There is an actual term for this experience, it's called "depersonalization." It comes with a few symptoms, but the one I experienced was the feeling that I was seeing my body or parts of my body from the outside. It was like I was floating in the air above myself. This condition is common in people who experience trauma or extreme stress. To say I was under a lot of stress when I experienced depersonalization would be a huge understatement.

So, let me take you to one of the most surreal and stressful times in my life. Coincidentally, it also happens to be right at the climax of my story. But why start here? Well, because while most stories build up to the life-changing moment, I'd need a whole book to share my backstory (hint: I'm writing another book wink, wink). Although what I'm about to reveal may sound like the biggest plot twist of all, this was just the beginning: So, let's get right to it. The day I was under so much stress, that my mind and body decided that it was too much to handle, that it tried to escape by floating above me, was the day I was sentenced to nineteen months in prison. Nope, you didn't read that wrong.

So, picture this: One moment, I'm planning my baby girl's milestone 1st birthday party, and the next, I'm standing in court, feeling like the world's worst mom, wife, and all-around worst person. My life turned upside down faster than you can say "plot twist." Suddenly, I was pulled from the familiar chaos of family and career life into a world where every choice was made for me (and that was just the tip of the iceberg as to the complexities of prison life). The reality of my transition was jarring. I was unrealistically praying for some sort of cinematic rescue or a dramatic change of heart by the judge. But as I lay in my cell, overwhelmed with worry, fear, and anxiety, and as days turned into weeks, and weeks into months, I realized that no one was coming to save me. It was time to pay my debt to society, own up to my mistakes, and begin the long, hard process of rescuing myself.

Because, unlike a movie, none of us can fast-forward to the end.

Now, maybe as soon as I revealed my story, your mind started racing, trying to piece together how I ended up in state prison. Let me set the record straight: No, I didn't physically hurt anyone, and I wasn't part of some bold heist. My fall from grace was a one-person job—just me—and it all revolved around money. As in, I was stealing money. There I was: a trusted employee by day, but secretly skimming cash from the company on the side. It might sound like the plot of a crime drama, but this was my reality. Stealing money isn't any less of a crime than violence or a heist; it's just a different kind of wrong. I'm not here to make excuses or shift the blame. I created this mess all by myself, and it was a colossal one.

The Reality of Rock Bottom

Rock bottom has a distinctive feel—cold, lonely, and unforgiving. It also has a sound, and for me, that sound was silence. In those first terrifying nights, the silence was deafening. It was just me, my never-ending thoughts, and the piercing realization of my new reality. Sometimes, I'd lay awake all night replaying how I got here. Other times, I'd try to sleep my reality away, hoping to wake up reunited with my family and the life I left behind. Being stripped of everything familiar was a brutal teacher.

> Rock bottom isn't a place you visit;
> it's a place you endure.

Every day in prison started the same way: the unmistakable sound of the metal cell door slamming, the guards' keys hitting against their legs as they walked, the single file shuffle to the cafeteria for meals, the unending routine, the constant feeling of uneasiness with each passing minute. The sameness was suffocating. I found myself longing for any distraction, any way to break the monotony. Books and writing became my escape. I devoured everything I could get my hands on, from self-help to fiction to business books. Each book was a temporary escape from my new reality. I also wrote every day to my family and friends, at times to myself, and other times I wrote to the universe, anything to keep my mind occupied.

> Because prison is likely everything you've
> seen in movies and TV shows, plus so much more
> that they don't show.

The Characters Along the Way

Every journey, especially those with unexpected detours, has characters who leave a lasting impact. If it's not already evident, let me be absolutely clear: prison isn't funny, and what landed me there is even less so. But to survive, I had to find light in my ongoing saga because the alternative was much more terrifying. I chose to see my sentence as a forced (albeit very deserved) time for soul-searching.

I met people from all walks of life, some familiar with the criminal justice system and some, like me, there for the first time. Faces and names blur together, but some people are unforgettable. Some were mothers, daughters, and sisters, but each with their own stories, their own pain. In my darkest days, the women I shared that bleak space with became my support system, my unexpected friends, and surprisingly, sometimes my source of laughter and wisdom. Life's detours have a way of introducing us to people who challenge our preconceptions, and add depth to our stories in ways we could never have anticipated.

Among them, a woman who became more of a kindred spirit. We went through a traumatic experience together, and that bond is hard to break. No one understands what you've been through quite like someone who went through it alongside you. We're bonded for life, and she'll always be a friend for life.

There was also a grandmother, who had made the ultimate mistake of drinking while driving—a decision that resulted in a tragic accident, leading to the loss of innocent lives. If you've ever had an alcoholic beverage, even just one, and gotten behind the wheel of a car, please hold your judgment. Despite the weight of her past, she reminded me that I, too, deserved a second chance. She had a tough exterior, but underneath, she possessed a gentle soul. She would often share stories of her life, her children, and her grandkids with a wistful smile. I could write several chapters about the women I met during that time, each of whom played a part in helping me come through the other side of my experience—more humbled and more forgiving of myself and others.

There was an incident that occurred after I came home. I was speaking with an old mentor of mine, and she said she wanted to be honest with me. She mentioned that it seemed like I had treated my sentence more like a sabbatical. She felt she could tell me this because she was one of the people I wrote to in my attempt to escape my newfound reality.

From all the letters I sent her, she walked away feeling as though I didn't fight hard enough to come home—that I sounded a little too optimistic for someone paying her debt for her crime in prison. She continued by saying that had she been in my position, she would have fought tooth and nail to return to her husband, children, and life in general—something she felt I didn't try to do. To her, it appeared as though I used my time as an extended vacation, especially when I mentioned that I had taken up running and writing as ways to cope. She was, as everyone is, entitled to her opinion. But the lesson I took away from her observation was that nobody can really know what someone is going through unless they have walked in their shoes.

Not many people knew that in the first few months of my sentence, I utilized the prison's law library (yes, the prison had a law library) to its fullest extent. On my own, I filed several court proceedings. I requested a retrial, asked for a different judge to oversee my case, sought to be re-sentenced, asked for my felony classification to be reclassified, and as a last resort, I even requested house arrest. All of these requests were DENIED. For my own sanity, I chose to remain hopeful as much as I could. Believe me, there were many moments when I wasn't as positive, and I let my fears and worries consume me for days and weeks at a time. But I found hope in writing and running, and I'm so grateful I discovered ways to keep my head above water. The idea that just because I sounded optimistic in my writing meant I wasn't trying to find ways to come home, or that I wasn't taking my situation seriously, is misguided.

> Optimism and depression can, and often do, coexist—they are not mutually exclusive.

The people I met inside those walls had their own stories. I had no more right to judge them than someone reading my hopeful letters had the right to assume I hadn't taken my situation seriously. When she shared her perspective on my time away, I realized it wasn't my responsibility to reason with her. I didn't need to convince her that I was doing all I could to come home, or that I certainly wasn't treating prison like "Club Med," as she described it. The only people who needed to know I had done all I could were myself, my then-husband, and, later on, when she was old enough to understand, my daughter.

Lessons in Unlikely Places

Prison teaches a person many things, but for me, the greatest lesson was resilience. It's a trait I believe we all possess, and when we find ourselves in the depths of our worst experiences, resilience rises to the occasion. In those 19 months, I learned more about empathy, forgiveness, and resilience than I had in all the years leading up to them. Each day was a lesson in survival, not just physically, but emotionally and mentally. I was learning to survive my own guilt, to confront the terrible decisions I had made, and to find a way to face my future.

Isolation forces you to either avoid the elephant in the room or confront it head-on. For a while, I focused on avoidance, doing everything I could to dodge the hard work of self-reflection. But in the silence, I was forced to face the toughest audience of all: myself. I had to come to terms with the choices that led me there, to own them and understand them. It was a process of peeling back layers of denial, trying to justify my actions (even though there was no justification), and eventually reaching forgiveness and acceptance.

Because, no matter how hard I tried,
I couldn't undo the past.

The Messy Art of Rebuilding

I will never forget the day I finally came home. I had marked each day I was away on my calendar with a big X. Not only did I cross the days off, but I also kept a count of the days as they passed, a total of 578 days. Even looking at that number today, I can feel a lump forming in my throat. 578 days is just four months shy of two years. At exactly nineteen months to the day I left, I was finally home.

But "home" was like stepping into a life that vaguely resembled my old one, yet belonged to someone else. Everything seemed the same, however nothing truly was. When I left, I was a newlywed, a new mom, and had just been promoted to a position I worked hard for. Coming home, I was facing a divorce, co-parenting my nearly three-year-old, jobless, homeless, broke, and with a résumé gap I couldn't easily explain.

My new reality was difficult to face. I put on a happy face for myself and my daughter but inside I was drowning. My time away had allowed me to hide in the shadows of my bad choices. Returning home, I had to face the music and I felt judged by everyone. I avoided places where I might run into people I knew, and I kept conversations light. Questions like, "Where have you been?" were answered with, "Oh, you know, around." I would then find a quick way to change the subject. I trusted no one, not even myself. What I didn't know at the time was I had slowly begun building my own kind of prison, just without the armed guards and barbed wire fences.

Solitude became my refuge, but what I didn't know I desperately needed was a trusted community.

I was incredibly lucky to find a job that provided the bare essentials and overlooked the "gap" in my résumé. This job gave me a roof over my head and food on the table. I'm grateful for my immediate family and a small circle of close friends who were my lifeline for emotional, mental, and financial support. During this time, I was reluctant to form new connections. Making new friends as an adult is already challenging, and my complex past made it seem even more daunting. Unsure of who I could trust, I initially kept my life very private. However, my fear of ridicule and judgment meant that I started stretching the truth about why my marriage broke up, the gap in my résumé and where I'd been for nearly two years. Once again, it felt like I was back to square one, hiding and masking the truth.

Then one day, I unexpectedly found myself sharing small bits and pieces of my story with a woman I had become close to at work. It took hours to put what I had been through into words, and even then, I couldn't share all the broken pieces. But with each small piece I shared, I began to feel a different kind of freedom.

From Isolation to Connection

What started as a moment of vulnerability turned into something I never expected. Little did I know, the woman I opened up to was part of a small circle of women who were on their own journey of healing and were eager to share their own stories and hear mine. That connection led me to a larger network of female entrepreneurs, each on their own path of discovery. Our shared need for community, sisterhood, and storytelling pushed me to open up even more. What began as casual meetups soon became regular networking dinners, which eventually turned into meaningful partnerships and collaborations.

Before this chapter of my life, I had spent two decades climbing the corporate ladder, surrounded by inspiring yet fiercely competitive women. I had my close group of girlfriends, but let's be honest—when you're living a double life, no one gets to know the real you. Heck, I didn't even know the real me. My corporate life felt like an endless race, with everyone trying to outdo each other to reach the top. Finding this new circle of women, where genuine support and openness were the norm, was a game changer. I went from keeping my life private to laying it all out on the table—mistakes, regrets, and everything in between. Sharing the raw, real stuff—our dreams, failures, and fears—became my new way of forming genuine connections.

The joy of connecting through stories was a revelation. I had spent so long hiding parts of myself (I didn't even know existed) that opening up felt scary, but also like a breath of fresh air. The women I met through this network became my circle. We laughed, cried, embraced our unique journeys, and supported each other through our losses. For the first time in a long while, I felt truly seen and understood.

Those early months of trying to shed the masks I had worn for years—masks that allowed me to pretend to be someone I wasn't—were incredibly tough. But I knew that if I was going to go through the hard work of sharing my truth, putting those masks back on would be pointless. Little did I know, I was starting to plant the seeds that would eventually become the foundation of my business.

Guilt, Grief, and Gratitude

Even as I soaked up the joy of my new life, I was sharing my story mainly for my own healing. It felt like a release, slowly peeling back the layers I had kept hidden for so long. But navigating through this wasn't easy—there were still parts of my story I hadn't come to terms with. The emotions that kept bubbling up to the surface were a complex mix of guilt, grief, and gratitude.

The guilt over the choices that led to my imprisonment was relentless, followed by deep grief for the life I left behind, especially the missed milestones of my daughter's early years, the strained relationships, the loss of trust and credibility, and the years I can never get back. Yet, as I shared my story, I began to find a way through the spiral of self-blame.

Opening myself up to share my deepest fears and biggest failures, became my light at the end of the tunnel. It taught me the power of real vulnerability and how to turn my most painful experiences into strengths. Through this humbling journey, I learned that while grief and guilt are heavy, they can also be transformative. I was pushed to reflect, to grow, to accept, and not just survive but also find the strength to keep moving forward.

Even today, as I face life's many challenges, my journey is a reminder that I can do hard things.

Gratitude comes in many forms. One particularly powerful moment came when I shared my story on stage for the first time. After growing comfortable sharing my stories in small groups, I was invited to speak on a panel about authenticity in business. With a shaky voice and tears on the verge of spilling over, I shared how I had redefined myself and how owning and accepting my past was a crucial part of my reinvention. As I spoke, I noticed tears in the eyes of some of the women in the audience. At first, I thought they were crying for me, but I soon realized they were crying for themselves. Afterward, several of the women I had seen emotionally moved by what I shared approached me to tell their own stories of struggle, survival, and trauma-such as homelessness and abuse. That day, I began to realize just how powerful our collective stories could be, and I felt a deep sense of gratitude for the chance to hold space and give others permission to share their own experiences.

Blessings Disguised As Setbacks

Even though I was incredibly grateful to be employed, the time I spent within an expanding circle of inspiring women sparked my curiosity about what might come next for me. Most of my former colleagues had all but written me off, and even some immediate family members urged me to keep my past buried. At first, I agreed with them, it seemed easier to leave past mistakes in the past. Yet, every morning as I drove to work, a sense of dread settled in.

The idea of storytelling as a career felt far-fetched. At that time, I couldn't think of a single person who made a living by telling stories (well, except for Oprah, but who could compete with that?). My dreams of wanting more were overshadowed by the practical reality that I needed a job. After all, I was now a single mom, and starting my own business didn't seem like a realistic possibility for someone in my position. Then, in a surprising twist, the universe intervened. One day, at the end of a workday, my boss informed me that my position was being eliminated due to budget cuts. I was unfortunately the last one hired, so I was the first to go.

At that moment, I once again found myself back at rock bottom, without so much as a backup plan.

On the outside, I was understandably anxious and scared. But buried deep down, my soul was doing cartwheels. Left to my own devices, I might have clung to that job for years, paralyzed by the fear of the unknown. Being laid off, though frightening, turned out to be an unexpected blessing—it opened a new chapter and led to the creation of my business.

Embracing My Superpower

Starting a new business is exciting, but the thrill didn't last long. I have worked for large corporations and small companies, achieving great success in all my roles. But owning your own business brings complexities that not many people talked about back when I started nearly 10 years ago. Today, I'm thankful for entrepreneurs who openly share the rollercoaster that is entrepreneurship. My early years of running my business mirrored my early days of freedom: filled with lots of hope and optimism but also dotted with more missteps than I could count. The notion of "If you build it they will come" became my goal post. However, without a clear sense of who I was and what I stood for, all my efforts felt, at best, disjointed and unsustainable, and at worst, disastrous and unsuccessful.

Don't get me wrong—I had some level of success in the beginning. But it came at a cost: burnout, misguided focus, misaligned clients, and the nagging feeling that I needed to be like everyone else who seemed successful on the outside. In those early years, I didn't always know who I was or what I stood for, and that led to some mistakes. I made decisions that didn't align with my values, didn't deliver on promises, and, as a result, let people down. It's something I deeply regret, but it also became a catalyst for my growth. These experiences pushed me to realign with my true values and to build a business that reflects who I am at my core.

Around this time, I hired well-intentioned mentors and coaches who advised me that *storytelling* wasn't scalable. They told me to focus on the right marketing strategies, sales offers, funnel structures, brand design—you name it. Know that I don't discount the importance of those strategies; they are all crucial for successfully growing a business. But I often overlooked what truly set me apart: *My Story*.

> And storytelling, the very thing that ignited my passion and lit up my soul, was my ultimate superpower.

After more than three years of chasing every trend, listening to mentors who dismissed storytelling, mimicking others' strategies, and working with clients who weren't the right fit, I made a pivotal decision. This time, I doubled down on what truly brought me so much joy: *Stories*. It wasn't just about reigniting my passion for sharing my journey; it was about diving deep into the art of storytelling itself. I threw myself back into speaking, both virtually and in person, breathing new life into my stories and reconnecting with audiences on a level I had deeply missed. I launched my podcast, *Bounce Back Like A Badass*, creating a space where stories could flourish and resonate with people around the world. As my services transformed, so did I. A new version of myself emerged—one that was laser-focused on harnessing the power of storytelling.

With this newfound clarity, I rediscovered the spark that had first led me to entrepreneurship. Embracing who I was, flaws and all, was the missing piece of the puzzle. Stories, I realized, were more than just a passion or a business—they were the lens through which I understood the world and my unique place within it. By embracing this truth and realigning my business with storytelling at its core, I found where I truly belonged. This journey back to my "why," the heart of storytelling, reminded me that the most powerful tool an entrepreneur can possess is true authenticity. In a world overflowing with viral trends, one-size-fits-all solutions, and overnight success stories, our personal journeys shine as timeless connections to genuine authenticity

Finding Beauty in the Mess

As I sit here, reflecting on my journey from the depths of humiliation and despair to personal and professional fulfillment, I realize that my story is far from over. In fact, it's just beginning.

To anyone reading this and wondering if your story matters, let me assure you: it absolutely does. Your story is uniquely yours—valuable and irreplaceable.

> It's in the mess of our experiences that the most meaningful beauty can emerge.

I once heard someone say that our gift or purpose often sits right next to the worst thing that's ever happened to us. I've found that to be true in my own life. So own your unique story, share it, and watch as it transforms into something more powerful and beautiful than you ever imagined.

I invite you to look at your own life experiences from a new perspective. If you're ready to begin to embrace the power of your story, start by asking yourself these key questions as you embark on your own storytelling journey:

How to Start Owning Your Story

1. What pivotal moments have shaped who you are today?
2. How have your challenges and setbacks contributed to your growth?

3. What are the recurring themes in your life story?
4. What lessons have you learned from your failures?
5. How do you want your story to inspire others?
6. What aspects of your story have you been reluctant to share, and why?
7. What is the next chapter you want to write for your life?

Let these questions sink in, and let them guide you in crafting a story that is authentically yours.

> Remember, the power of your story lies in its truth and the courage it takes to own every part of it—the good, the bad, and (especially) the parts we keep hidden.

Unlock Your Story

To support you on this journey, I've created a free downloadable guide, "Unlock Your Story: A Workbook to Build a Genuine Business Through Your Personal Story." This resource is filled with exercises and thought-provoking questions to help you dive deeper into your story and unlock your full potential.

Download your free copy at www.catcoley.com and start owning your story today. When you sign up, you'll also receive regular insights, tips, and inspiration delivered straight to your inbox to keep you connected and motivated on your journey.

The Rest Is Still Unwritten

As we reach the end of this chapter, both literally and metaphorically, I raise my glass to the unwritten chapters of our lives. May they be filled with laughter, tears, and growth. May we have the courage to face our plot twists with grace, grit, and strength. And may we never forget the power of owning our stories, for they are the legacy we leave behind and the impact we dare to create.

My story is a testament to the power of embracing your mess. It's about finding the humor in the face of rock bottoms, about the resilience to start over, and the courage to say, "*This is me, flaws and all.*" So, to anyone out there feeling like their life resembles a blooper reel more than a highlight reel, remember this:

There's Beauty in the Mess. Embrace it. Own it.

I have so many people to be grateful for, including my immediate family and close friends, who have been a constant source of love and support. To my daughter, my true north, and the inspiration behind every dream I chase—you give me the courage to move through my fears and reach beyond my wildest dreams. My deepest gratitude to my sister, my saving grace, my angel on earth—you've been my rock, my strength, and the one who always sees the light in me, even when I can't see it myself. And to the man who's been my partner through the thick of it—thank you for your patience, your encouragement, and your ability to cut through my bullshit and catch me when I slip up, as it often happens in life.

As I reflect on my journey and the people who have walked with me, I want to offer the same support to you. If you're ready to unpack your stories, I'd be honored to walk alongside you in your storytelling journey. Let's create your own unforgettable real-life indie movie. Thank you for allowing me to share mine.

With heartfelt gratitude,
Cat

Annie Mirza

Founder and CEO of Sensus Social

www.linkedin.com/in/anniemirza
https://www.facebook.com/anniemirzacpa
https://www.instagram.com/annie_mirza_cpa
https://sensus.social/
https://www.anniemirza.com

Annie Mirza is a CPA turned digital marketing strategist, website designer and a mindset coach for Accountants.

As the founder and CEO of Sensus Social, she coaches accountants on a holistic approach to building human focused digital firms that they can be proud to leave as their legacy.

Her transition from a burned-out accountant to a successful online business strategist serves as a testament to her commitment to reshaping the accounting industry norms. Annie's mission is to show accountants there's another way to build a firm that gives you freedom of time, money, and purpose.

Outside of her role as CEO at Sensus Social, Annie's passions are just as multifaceted and include writing fiction, training for a TaeKwondo black belt, embarking on exciting family adventures across the world, spending Saturdays with her parents, and trying, albeit at times unsuccessful, to learn how to ski with her kids.

A Moment in Time

By Annie Mirza

Life is lived in moments, defined by actions, reactions, or inactions, and remembered mostly in fondness.

Before I wrote a single word of this chapter, I pondered for a long time what I wanted my reader to get from this. I have lived, as most of us have, a complicated life. When I look back on my journey, I can clearly see the moments that defined my trajectory, the actions, reactions, and inactions that shaped me to be who I am today. These things involve not only me but everyone around me, which by the way, includes strangers. Why then do so many of us think that we don't matter?

I suppose I want to say before I get into my story that we, knowingly or unknowingly, affect each other's lives. Words are powerful because we assign meanings to them as we receive them. How much of my story resonates with you, if at all, will hugely depend on your state of mind. So, allow yourself to contemplate what comes up. You may dismiss what you read or you may be enthralled. Whatever happens, my prayer is that you receive whatever you need in the moment as you read these words. For what we seek is seeking us and we shall receive it when we open our minds to it.

I invite you to think for a moment, what is it that I seek right now in my life? What would make me feel most fulfilled? It has nothing to do with monetary things, but so much to do with your whole being. I make no promises, but when you seek you often find it. Maybe it is not in the words you read, but you're here, you've picked up this book, and got this far into it.

From one human to another in search of meaning and purpose of life, for being here, right now at this moment in time, this is my story.

xxxx

"We don't need the lantern; the moonlight is so bright," I said to Yasir, my cousin, who was walking ahead of us holding a lantern and gently wobbling it from side to side. He was the gang leader. Three years older than me, and four years senior to my brother, Ali. The two of us marched behind him on a cobblestone gully, barely big enough for an ox cart to pass through. The houses towered over us in mud or stone walls blocking the blue light of the moon.

As we got closer to the end of the street into the open space, the moonlight beamed so bright you'd think a man was holding a blue torch above town. There was calming coolness in the air. The rain of the previous days helped lessen the summer heat significantly.

We could hear the running water in the shallow ravine that passed through the middle of town. People came to dump their trash at the base of it every night. When it rained heavily, the water would level with the small bridge and take the trash somewhere the villagers didn't have to worry about.

In that pile of trash, under the coolness of hanging trees, were blinking lights buzzing and moving like little stars that stirred when you stood still looking up after spinning too many circles. Fireflies. We were hunting these little treasures tonight. We tried to grab them in the palms of our hands.

"Careful, leave a little bit of a gap between your fingers so they can breathe," Yasir said. "We don't want to kill them."

"Wow! This one is blinking!"

"How do they light?"

"There's something on their tush that lights up?"

"But how?"

We inspected and contemplated these questions for a few minutes. None of us had satisfactory answers. Even Yasir, who was in fourth grade already, didn't know.

We kept trying to catch a few more before exploring what people had been dumping in the trash, and then discussing what else was beyond the path Ali and I had never crossed before.

This was a small rural town in Pakistan in 1987, and we were visiting our ancestral home where my dad grew up. He had built a brick house in a more convenient location which was closer to the city and public transportation. We would visit our ancestral home during the holidays to play with our cousins and visit our family farms with the elders during harvesting season.

Our home was next to the bus stop. All of our family members who lived at our ancestral home would stop by our home on the way to or from their destinations. It was always loud and buzzing with activity. In the coming years, our family multiplied from just me and Ali to four siblings and so did our cousins.

Often, all the cousins would gather at our home returning from someplace and nearly a dozen of us would march together in a herd from our home to the farms or our ancestral home singing loudly. We'd stop along the way exploring the open fields, carefully picking delicious cactus fruit while avoiding its infinitely invisible thorns, laughing at the lucky escapes of loose stray dogs, and chasing rainbows after it had rained.

My dad left home in search of a better life when I was four. My mom was a school teacher and she ran the household until my dad landed in the United States and found stability. While my mom worked, my grandma took care of us. She did the morning chores including cooking breakfast and lunch, cleaning, and all the visiting obligations such as weddings, funerals, sickness, and good fortunes of neighbors, friends, and, of course, relatives. My mom took on the responsibilities of afternoon and evening tasks. The two women lived harmoniously and that created a lot of balance, rhythm, and stability for the four of us growing up.

When it was just me and Ali, we visited our grandparents in the city every summer. While my grandma and uncles would be busy doing what adults do, our grandad would hang out with us. He was a military veteran. After serving in the military, he managed a small metal workshop attached to his home for many years. He eventually quit due to health reasons.

He had a cabinet next to his bed with all his medicine and little hakeemi (naturopathic) concoctions he made in his free time. He spent most of his days in bed, and we'd play around with him when we visited. He would play with us, throwing us in the air, rocking us on his legs, and playing magic tricks.

He would get us excited about squeezing the juice out of lemons to store for easy lemonade in the summer. He would tell us stories while rocking us in his rocking chair. He would take us to the kitchen and make his special curry when he didn't like what grandma had cooked. He would talk to us about God, people, life, and its expectations.

Ali was naughty (as most boys are at 2 or 3 years of age) and would get into his medicine cabinet. My grandad would tease him saying, "My baby girl will become a doctor and people will stand up for her when she passes. You will sell corn on a street cart." Ironically, my brother grew up to become a highly sought-after vascular surgeon and I became a CPA.

I was born in a country where men dominated the household, they made all the decisions, and they controlled the family dynamics. Women were supposed to simply follow. My grandfather was the one who gave me dreams. He told me I could be anyone I wanted to be. He taught me that I was no less than any man. I don't believe he repeated what he said to Ali, but I remember it vividly. It still reverberates in my mind. What's more powerful is that he didn't just say that to be malicious or to make my brother feel less. I believe it was an innocent statement. His actions, including how he raised my mother and my aunt, and how he treated other women in his life with ultimate respect are all examples of what he believed a woman deserved.

When I look back and reflect on my life, I held every man to that standard of manhood. If they didn't meet that standard then they weren't worthy of my respect. I remembered his words when things got tough as I entered the real world. His words were what gave me the confidence and belief to achieve all the amazing things I did in a male-dominated industry, i.e. accounting. Unfortunately, when other voices became louder, I lost myself to the darkness. But more on that later.

One summer day, when I was three and my brother was only two, we were visiting our grandparents. It was Ramadan and all the adults were fasting. My grandad had just left for the bazaar and had asked me what I wanted. I had told him, I wanted lots of mangoes.

We were playing in my grandparents' small courtyard when we heard a voice in the street.

"Come, get some ice cream! Ice cream with a cone!" sang the man in the street pushing a wooden cart with a metal drum in the center and hanging cones along the cart pillar. Ali and I pulled at our grandma's scarf, "We want ice cream! We want Ice cream!"

As the man's singing grew distant, our cries got louder.

This sort of thing was rare in our town. No one sold ice cream in carts on our streets. If we wanted ice cream, our mom either made it at home or bought it from the big shop in the city. Mom said no and Grandma tried to convince us that she'd buy it for us from the bazaar. She'd even take us to buy it, but we didn't budge. We had just heard the mesmerizing music of the ice cream man and there was no way we were going to ignore that.

Our grandma couldn't bear the cries, so she told my mom it was ok to buy us street food just once. They both wrapped their scarves around their heads, Mom picked up Ali and Grandma held my hand as we walked towards the singing voice.

We found him near the end of the street. Ali and I got a cone and started licking away. Ali didn't even finish the ice cream and tossed the cone aside. Meanwhile, I sat in my grandad's rocking chair in his shop and enjoyed every bit of deliciousness, including the crunchy, sweet wafer cone.

A short while later, the house became loud because Ali started to throw up. My mom and grandma tended to him, cleaning him up and figuring out what to give him to soothe his tummy.

I have glimpses of memories of what happened next, but I've been told the story by everyone in my family repeatedly that it feels like my own memories. A while after Ali, I started to throw up as well. But unlike him, I vomited blood. My mom and grandma took us both to the hospital immediately and called my aunt who was a nurse at the hospital.

Since Ali had thrown away the cone and vomited soon after, he was able to recover quickly. However, things didn't work out so well for me. Since I had enjoyed the entire ice cream cone and had a chance to digest it fully, the poison had penetrated deeper into my digestive tract. My stomach lining had been destroyed and I wouldn't stop throwing up blood. At first, doctors couldn't figure out what was going on. They gave me antibiotics, but I ended up with blood clots.

Eventually, they had to wash my stomach and give me two blood transfusions, one from my mom and one from my aunt's good friend who was also a nurse at the hospital my aunt worked at. My family still remembers fondly how she wanted to keep her fast while donating blood and everyone had to convince her otherwise. Your fast breaks when you donate blood. Allah doesn't burden the practice of faith.

My dad sobbed like a baby and cried for the mercy of Allah for the life of his daughter. He lost his temper at the poor old man who went around the streets banging metal and howling to wake up neighbors to get them up in time to prepare for morning meals before the break of dawn so they wouldn't miss their fasts. He didn't know I had just fallen asleep after hours of crying and puking blood clots.

Suffice to say, my whole family was rattled by this incident. My wishes became their command as I started to recover. I vividly remember one moment when my entire family, mom, dad, aunts, uncles, friends, and even a couple of neighbors were taking me somewhere in a hospital ward, they were reassuring my parents or me when I cried, "Our baby is going to be ok." "When you come out of surgery, I'll take you to the zoo," etc.

Grandad brought me mangoes every day for the whole summer and every summer after. He would tell me, "I will buy a mango so big for my baby girl, it will barely fit in one ox cart."

This was my first battle at being a survivor. I also believe this incident played a huge role in how my family treated me with unconditional love and affection. No matter what happened in life, (and so much did) my family was home, my safety, my blanket. I felt protected within the boundaries of our home.

From a very young age, I was a quiet child, more observant, and needing very little. However, I was called a sensitive child. If someone cried around me, I would start crying without understanding why they were crying. If a teacher yelled at another child, I would be upset for days but unable to understand or say anything to anyone. I believe because I was an easy-going child, when I got upset, adults around me would try to cheer me up. They didn't dismiss my sensitivity or get agitated. Unfortunately though, because of the label of a sensitive child, my opinions were dismissed when I became a young adult and then an adult.

What I learned late into my adulthood was that I'm an Empath. The sensitivity I've always had is because I'm highly attuned to other people's emotions and energies around me. This distinction would provide so much clarity and make a big difference in my healing from a long-term depression I would experience as an adult. We'll get to that soon.

Like I said before, life is lived in moments. Another moment that would change the trajectory of my life took place when I was only 8 years old. All of our cousins would come by our home, and we'd walk together to go to the bus stop for school. My siblings went to different schools, but I went to the same school as my cousins, which included four boys and one girl. As kids, we would ride the bus and often there weren't enough seats for us to sit on so we'd stand in the middle or sometimes, adults would ask the little ones to hop on their laps which made it easy for both, adults to have more legroom and kids to have rest.

It was one of those days when the bus was super packed and one of the men asked me to sit on his lap. Unfortunately, he had other intentions than just extra legroom. He molested me as I sat on his lap not thinking twice about what was going to happen. When I tried to jump off, he held me back firmly and I got scared. I wept quietly. When we got off the bus, my female cousin, who was also my classmate, asked me repeatedly why I was upset and I couldn't tell her the whole day. Finally, as she persisted, I told her that the man had touched me indecently. I probably wouldn't have had the courage to say anything to my mom, but my cousin told her mom, who then told my mom and grandma. They were all outraged. Since my dad wasn't around, my mom and grandma felt overprotective. They wanted to know who the man was, they wanted retribution. Of course, we never found out who he was because he wasn't from our town. Within a couple of days, my mom got us a private driver who would pick up my female cousin and me from our house and drop us off at the gate of our school. Yet again, I felt protected and loved even though my boundaries shrunk around me.

I remember being so angry. I remember pounding my fists at the concrete floor imagining what I would do to that man, or any man had they even tried so much as to look at me wrong. And I did. I beat up men in the bazaar who tried touching me. I beat up a man on the bus, wanting to break his leg because he had intentionally put it in my way as I tried to get off. Unfortunately, I learned later that I was hitting the femur which is apparently the strongest bone in the human body. Imagine my soreness when I realized there was no hope of breaking his leg. It stings to this day.

When you live in a country where it is considered normal for boys to harass girls by calling them pretty, asking their names, etc., it becomes a challenge to have to fight everyone. But after time I got better at picking my battles. I, like most girls, attracted too much unwanted attention and life became cumbersome outside the house. Once again, my family and my home became a sweet haven.

Then, at the age of 17, I moved to the United States with my family. You would think the move would've been difficult, but it was the opposite for me. My parents got me into college, taught me how to drive, got me a car and a phone, and sent me on my way. They trusted me with everything I did. From studying late at night in the library to going out with friends. I got scholarships to lower the financial burden on my parents and took part-time jobs when I felt I needed to contribute to the family financially.

If boys approached me for my phone number, I simply turned them down and appreciated the fact that I didn't have to fight them. They respected me enough to hear I wasn't interested. I spent four years in college and in those years, my confidence was sky-high. I landed my first job right after college at one of the big accounting firms. I helped my parents buy our first home in America. Ali and I planned in our free time how we were going to return to Pakistan to do something for our country and our people. I would write down plans in my journal on all the things I needed to do before I could make a meaningful impact. I envisioned approaching universities and building connections here in the United States that would allow more educational opportunities for my people back home. The American legal system, the great economy, business management, and practices, all were the things my country needed yesterday. I would dream and then dream some more.

Soon after I graduated and had worked at the accounting firm for six months, we went to Pakistan and I got married. My husband, MJ, was an IT professional, smart, and highly intelligent. He was offered jobs in several different countries around the world. He told me he didn't want people to think he married me because I was an American Citizen, so he wanted to live somewhere else. Of all the countries he had job offers, he asked me where I'd like to go. I picked Australia. This might sound terrible, but at the time, the only thing I knew of Australia was that it was a continent.

When MJ asked me this, my parents were still in Pakistan. They had gone for the whole two and half months of summer vacation with my younger siblings and only Ali and I had returned. I spoke with Ali about this, he said, "You should go! Start a new life somewhere alone."

So I did.

The move wasn't as exciting or easy as I dreamt it would be. Since the accounting firm I worked with had global offices, I simply asked them to transfer me to their Sydney office. It took a few phone calls, but I moved alongside MJ with a job that paid well. Easy, right?

Not!

When things go wrong, they go wrong in a domino effect. Imagine having to adjust to a new country and different culture without a family blanket to support you. My work was competitive, demanding, and involved multimillion, sometimes multibillion-dollar brands. I was also navigating a new, intimate relationship that I'd never experienced before and had the responsibilities of managing a household which was also new to me.

If I stop to think for a moment, this is enough to rattle anyone. The physical, psychological, and emotional needs of this new life overwhelmed me so much that I began to believe I wasn't smart enough, clever enough, or good enough in all areas of my life, all at once. In hindsight, this was the beginning of my depression which started to take root slowly like an oak tree.

I worked as an external auditor and took my job seriously. I worked extensively long hours, producing quality work in an environment where chargeable hours were a priority. If a job required more work and a partner didn't have the guts to stand up to the client and say we need to up our fees, because it's more work, they would write off the cost internally. If your job was written off more than others, you got dinged for it in more ways than was visible to anyone.

I had lived a sheltered life, untouched by the chaos and political nonsense of the outside world. I only knew what was right and what was wrong. Up until this point, I had not learned the world could look so gray that you'd find yourself lost in the fog. When it became too much to handle, I resorted to switching jobs, but it didn't help much. I lacked what I could never learn or develop, a manipulative mind and a sense of exchanging values and integrity for peace and security. I persisted in excelling solely on grit and perseverance, not knowing any better.

When it was time to have kids, I decided to leave that world to never look back. I couldn't envision raising a family with the life that I had been living.

When your heart is set on living on purpose, to make even a slight dent in the universe, living in isolation, raising toddlers, no matter how great and satisfying that is, eventually wears out and your soul yearns for more.

One day while folding laundry, a story popped into my head. I started to write. The small scene turned into a full-blown manuscript of a fiction novel in merely 4 weeks. The story of a young Pakistani girl who was molested at the age of 8 and how that single moment changed the trajectory of her life.

Sounds familiar?

I didn't see it at first, but as I started to edit the manuscript, it took me deep into my memories. Memories I had buried in my subconscious. When scabs peeled off and wounds turned raw again, I realized how much that moment had affected my ability to be who I was and could have been. More than anything else, it had robbed me of my self-worth. I had accomplished great things in life but that was through sheer confidence and willpower. When my self-worth had been put to the test, I allowed others to dim my light.

As much as writing that novel pushed me deep into depression, it also proved to be a catalyst for healing. I found a new purpose in life, a new passion. My soul lit up. I went back to school to study creative writing and published several short stories in anthologies. I got my manuscript assessed for publishing but when the editor asked me to pass it on to the publishers, I resisted. I didn't think I was ready emotionally to stand by my book and support it. It's still sitting in my computer, professionally edited and ready to be published. Maybe next year.

I didn't want to self-publish the book because I believed the story was too important and needed the backing of a professional book publisher to support it. When I started searching for publishing agents, I learned that people with personal brands and the following had a much better chance of getting a contract. So I told myself I needed to learn how to build a personal brand and learn marketing first. Ah, the stories we tell ourselves when our soul resists.

When I moved back to the United States, I decided to start my own business, but not in accounting. I had so much PTSD, I didn't want to have anything to do with that industry. By that time, MJ and I had a successful IT consulting business. MJ also built a great app he was trying to market without much success, and the idea of building a personal brand to publish my very first novel seemed enthralling. MJ suggested I start a marketing agency. The only problem was, I didn't know the first thing about marketing. So, I did what I've always done. I dove in headfirst.

When I first started the business in marketing, I was clinically depressed, on antidepressants, and unable to eat much of anything due to chronic gut issues. Because of the move to the United States, I lost one good psychologist I had finally found in Sydney. I had only a few powerful sessions with her, but she had helped put back together the pieces of my courage and confidence.

I spent the first year of my business learning marketing but more importantly, healing my depression through mindset strategies. I spent hours trying to remap my brain to remind myself of who I truly was. Being back in a place where I had so much success and being close to my family helped remind me of what I was capable of.

Slowly, I found myself again and started to establish my business. However, at every corner, I was met with this gnawing reality that I needed to serve the accounting industry. It was my specialty and my niche. My friends still in the accounting industry told me they needed my services. The industry relied heavily on referrals, which wasn't effective for exponential growth. They had no idea how to market themselves and their businesses. The profession was also struggling with an image problem both for recruitment of talent and attracting clients who valued their services. Still, I wasn't convinced I could return.

It wasn't until I witnessed online businesses making millions of dollars shut down due to poor finance management and a lack of systems and processes. That was the moment I realized that accountants are not needed, they are necessary for the survival of a capitalist economy. The entire world depends on this economy. The failure of one industry could have severe consequences as we had witnessed in 2008 with the Global Financial Crisis.

Finally, in 2023, I wrote my mission statement, "Empowering Accountants to Build Human-Focused Firms." I began volunteering at the Nevada Society of CPAs and connected with industry influencers and decision-makers to understand what was going on in the industry. I spent many hours speaking with accountants to figure out what they were struggling with and what was the best way to help them.

Now, in 2024, I am crafting new offers and services specifically addressing the problems many accountants face. I want to reimagine the industry by equipping these heartfelt leaders with the tools they need to truly succeed at making an impact that not only serves companies but people within them.

My journey from being a little empathic girl who suffered from food poisoning to molestation to migration across oceans thrice, I may add, has truly come full circle. I am still a work in progress as I recently realized how my childhood trauma has been affecting my ability to fully show up online. Though I would have never believed it consciously, deep down it has crippled me with self-worth issues. I have kept from fully owning my genius and sharing it with the world. Self-doubts like people wouldn't listen to me when there are louder voices than mine. I will run this offer when I have perfected my own website.

I better learn a little more about TikTok as some of my clients may be using it. Lies! All Lies! There are countless things that go through our heads unnoticed, but stay in our subconscious keeping us stuck.

I'm currently working on remapping my brain to believe that I am worth everything that God has blessed me with. That I'm not only a CPA, but also a great marketer, a brilliant writer, and a passionate human being who genuinely cares about people. No one can create like I can because no one in this world has the same dreams and passions that I have. I am worthy of standing before others and telling my story because, believe it or not, we each have a story to tell and every single one of our stories is worth hearing.

So go on and tell *your* story. Tell it to your friends and family, share it on social media, go on stages or podcasts! Use your voice because the moment we voice whatever it is we've allowed to take hold of our powers, it loses its hold. No matter what life has thrown at you, I promise you that you are more powerful to overcome those challenges. You can do it! I believe in YOU! Be YOU!

To help you get started in building your own brand online, download my free <u>Website Launch Planner & Checklist</u> at <u>https://sensus.social/website-launch-planner-checklist</u>.

For Accountants, check out <u>Sensus Social</u> for more resources on building a brand online. For online entrepreneurs, check out <u>BildaSite</u> for websites that build your business.

Alexis Enterline

Half Moon Mental Health and Wellness
Clinical Social Worker and Mindset Coach

https://www.linkedin.com/in/alexisenterline/
https://www.facebook.com/groups/thelifelab
https://www.instagram.com/alexis.enterline/
https://halfmoonmentalhealthandwellness.com/
https://www.alexisenterline.com/

Alexis is a dedicated expert in women's mental health and wellness, inspired to enter the field in 2007 after facing her own mental health hurdles. Her personal journey ignited a deep passion for empowering others to overcome similar challenges. When she's not immersed in a good book or exploring new destinations, Alexis is committed to helping her clients break through barriers to their mental and emotional well-being. She offers a tailored approach that holistically addresses the mind, body, and spirit, ensuring that each client receives care that resonates with their unique needs. Discover more about Alexis's transformative methods and how she can guide you towards achieving your wellness goals at alexisenterline.com.

From Struggle to Strength

By Alexis Enterline

My story is one you might find familiar. It is a story about the search for belonging, understanding, and ultimately, a way to help others through my own struggles.

Seeking Acceptance in the World

I grew up in a home where there was a lot of love, but obedience was the expectation. Even with all the love, I often felt like an outsider looking in. Questions weren't encouraged, and the usual answer to any "why" was "because I said so." Any challenge to this statement was met with a swift whack on the leg with a spatula or the threat of my dad and his belt later on. My sister seemed to naturally fit in wherever she went, and I viewed her as the family favorite. I, however, retreated into my own world, feeling more and more out of place. I felt like I looked different, acted different, and just did not belong anywhere or with anyone.

Our family's financial situation was very modest growing up. We lived in an old farmhouse, and I was very aware of how different our financial reality was compared to others in our circle. My mom was a stay-at-home mom and my dad was a factory foreman. While my classmates seemed to enjoy a comfortable life, I learned to make do with what we had. These differences were subtle but deeply affected how I saw myself and interacted with the world. This reality was subtle but highlighted by my exclusion from social activities; I was rarely invited to birthday parties or after-school events, reinforcing my sense of detachment and impacting my self-esteem.

I remember a particular incident vividly. During a sixth-grade class play, I secretly hoped to be cast as one of the pretty girls in the Western theme theater production we were doing. It was a role that signified to me acceptance and inclusion with the rest of the girls. Every other girl in the class was cast in this way so I was sure that I would be too. I was shocked when my teacher decided I would play the gunslinger, Kate. She was described as loud and brash. Overwhelmed by a sense of shame that I was seen this way, I sunk even further into myself. All I wanted was to be included and this casting served as yet another reminder to me that I didn't fit into the mold.

As I transitioned into adolescence, my efforts to fit in intensified. I experimented with smoking, and drugs, and entered into early sexual relationships. Each decision was a misguided attempt to feel accepted by those around me. These choices were cries for connection and recognition. However, the arrival of my first daughter while I was still a teenager marked a critical turning point in my life. Suddenly, the stakes were higher, and the need to find a better path for both myself and my daughter became my main focus.

This new responsibility caused me to reevaluate my life and my goals. I needed to create an environment for my daughter that differed from my own —an environment where questions were welcomed and where feeling different was not just accepted but encouraged. This pivot not only altered my personal life but also set the stage for my future career, where I would dedicate myself to helping others navigate their feelings of otherness and transform them into sources of empowerment.

Despite the love I received from my family, the mix of strict rules and financial strain created a complicated emotional environment. The feeling of being different, coupled with a constant awareness of our financial limitations, taught me resilience. It also sparked a determination to create a different path for myself, one where I could question, explore, and ultimately build a life without the restrictions I experienced growing up.

These early experiences, though tough, became the foundation of my perseverance. They taught me the value of hard work, the importance of empathy, and the need to forge my own identity. Looking back, I can see how these formative years equipped me with the strength to handle life's challenges, including the intense struggles I faced later on as a mother and professional.

In many ways, my childhood struggles to find acceptance and belonging were the preparation for the work I would eventually embrace. They taught me the importance of empathy, the value of diverse perspectives, and the crucial role of supportive relationships in overcoming adversity. As I moved forward, these lessons became the foundation of my approach to women's mental health, influencing how I engage with clients and guide them toward healing and self-acceptance.

From Personal Struggles to Professional Insights

The quest to find myself and help others led me to social work and then to specialize in women's mental health. Each step, from my difficult adolescence to confronting the harsh realities of my clients' traumas, sharpened my resolve to find healing methods that embraced the whole person—mind, body, and spirit.

My first encounter with social work was personal—I needed a social worker's help as a young, newly single mom. I got married at 19 and was divorced by 22. By the time of my divorce, I had completed my Bachelor's degree in Psychology and was working full-time. However, my income wasn't enough to support myself and my daughter, so I sought public assistance. The process was incredibly challenging. It felt like every step was met with roadblocks, and I often felt judged as if I were trying to cheat the system.

During this tough time, while figuring out my next steps, I discovered the field of social work. This was a turning point for me. I vowed to enter a helping profession where I could ensure that people seeking help would never feel the shame and embarrassment I experienced. I went on to earn my Master's Degree in Social Work and immediately started working in the field, focusing on helping families.

Over the past two decades as a social worker, I've primarily worked with children, families, and women. It's been a journey filled with challenges and triumphs, but the work I've done with women stands out the most. I've seen firsthand the transformative power of providing support and resources to women in need. The impact has been profound, not only on their lives but also on mine. Each success story reinforces my belief in the importance of compassion and understanding in social work.

Helping women navigate their challenges and find their strength has been the most rewarding aspect of my career. Their resilience inspires me every day, and their successes keep me inspired. My experiences have come full circle, from needing help to providing it, and I am deeply committed to making a positive difference in the lives of those I serve.

Empowering Others Through Shared Experience

After the birth of my first daughter, I was overwhelmed by intense feelings of sadness and a lack of motivation. I didn't understand these new emotions and felt lost. Seeking help, I visited my primary care doctor and described my symptoms. She diagnosed me with postpartum depression and prescribed an antidepressant, suggesting I follow up "if I felt the need." As I left the room with my daughter, I overheard her mocking me to her medical assistant. This experience shattered my trust, and I threw away the prescription, convinced that my feelings were invalid if even my doctor ridiculed them.

When my daughter's father and I separated, my depression and sense of worthlessness deepened. Once again, I could not fit in and was left alone. This time though, I was also responsible for another human being. I clung to a clear vision of what I did not want our lives to become, which propelled me forward. I struggled through school, navigated the challenges of dating with mixed (mostly bad) experiences, and constantly facing financial hardships. I told myself that once I graduated and landed an incredible job, all my struggles would end. This was a lie.

Working in public service revealed harsh realities: the pay is low, the emotional toll is high, and burnout is a constant threat. I had to develop new skills to support myself while caring for others, be present for my daughter despite witnessing unspeakable things, and manage an entirely new level of stress. All the while, I felt pressured by societal expectations that, as a woman, I should handle everything without complaint.

As I gained experience, I realized that the common beliefs about boundaries, expectations, and being a woman were flawed. This awareness allowed me to chart a new path for myself, one that I began to model for others.

Balancing the demands of my career with the responsibilities of motherhood was not an easy task. I often found myself working long hours, juggling the needs of my clients with those of my young daughter. There were countless late nights and early mornings, trying to fit in quality time with her between case notes and home visits. I would learn new therapeutic techniques in training classes and then practice them at home with my daughter. I missed important school events because I was afraid of losing my job if I asked for the time off to attend. I felt pulled in so many directions, I did not know how I was going to manage most days. Despite the exhaustion, I was determined to succeed both as a professional and as a mom.

During this challenging period, I met someone who would become a significant part of my life. Finding a new partner brought a fresh wave of hope and support. With him, I discovered a new level of companionship, which eventually led to the joy of becoming a mom again. This time, I was more prepared, more resilient, and more aware of my own needs and boundaries. However, I still struggled with the "balance" of personal and professional life. It was during this time that I started to realize that the idea of balance is a myth. There can never be a full balance. I embraced the idea of flow. There are times in life when your family will need you more and times when your professional priorities will take precedence. It is important to find the flow, like a wave, within that so that it begins to feel more manageable. I was starting to really embrace this flow in the spring of 2020. I had decided to start saying no to more offers in order to truly align myself with my values. Life then decided it would throw me another curveball.

The summer of 2020 was a season of profound loss and heartache for me. Within just four months, I experienced the deaths of both of my parents. First, my mom passed away, leaving a void that felt insurmountable. Just as I was beginning to process that loss, my dad followed. The grief was overwhelming, and it felt like the ground had been pulled out from under me. I had come far in my relationship with my parents and felt cheated by life that just as I was feeling good, they were taken from me.

Navigating this grief during a global pandemic added so many layers of isolation. Traditional ways of mourning and finding solace in the company of loved ones were no longer possible. In those first weeks, I often felt like I was drifting through a fog, barely able to function. The responsibilities of daily life seemed insurmountable, and the weight of my grief was compounded by feeling alone. I felt abandoned by people I thought of as friends, I felt like people in my daily life did not understand what I was going through, and I felt the need to hold it together as best I could for my daughters. I allowed myself to cry and grieve with my girls as I wanted them to know that this was okay but I did not want to rely on them to support me. I knew I had to find a new way to navigate my sorrow and rebuild my sense of stability.

Through this journey, I learned to navigate grief in a new way. It was not about moving on or forgetting what had happened but about finding ways to integrate my loss into my life. It is still there every single day. I allowed myself to feel the pain, to cry, and to mourn, but also to celebrate the love and memories that would always be a part of me. I discovered that grief is not a linear process but a continuous one, with waves that ebb and flow over time. My previous beliefs on flow were reinforced during this time. There were days when the pain was raw and overwhelming, and others when fond memories brought a bittersweet smile to my face. Embracing this ebb and flow became essential to my continued healing.

The experience of losing both parents reshaped my understanding of resilience and the importance of community and chosen family. It reinforced the necessity of leaning on others, of being vulnerable, and of finding personal ways to honor and remember our loved ones. In the midst of the greatest sorrow I had ever known, I found a new depth of strength and an unwavering determination to carry forward with love and compassion.

Forming and nurturing a supportive community became essential in my journey through grief. In the past, I had often felt the pressure to handle things on my own, to be strong and self-reliant. But the loss of my parents made it clear that true strength lies in our connections with others. I found a group of like-minded women who provided a safe space where I could express my emotions without fear of judgment. They listened, offered comfort, and shared their own stories of loss, creating shared experiences that made me feel less alone. Grief and loss is not just about death. I discovered it could also be about the loss of expectations of what we thought life would look like.

This community reminded me of the importance of being vulnerable. By opening up about my struggles and allowing others to support me,

I found a sense of solidarity and understanding that was healing. It taught me that asking for help is not a sign of weakness but a testament to our need for human connection. In turn, I became more attuned to the needs of those around me, offering my own support and empathy to others facing similar challenges.

The strength of a community lies in its ability to lift each other up, to provide a network of support that can help us navigate the darkest times. My parents' deaths brought an overwhelming sense of loss, but the community I had built offered a light in that darkness. They helped me to see that even in the midst of profound sorrow, there can be moments of joy, connection, and hope.

These personal experiences deepened my empathy and understanding, making me a better social worker and therapist. I saw the impact of my work not just in my clients' lives but also in my own. By sharing my journey and the lessons I learned along the way, I was able to inspire others to break free from societal expectations and create their own paths.

Today, as I reflect on my journey, I am proud of the woman I have become. I have faced immense challenges and found strength in the love and support of those around me. My experiences have taught me that while life can be incredibly tough, it is also filled with moments of profound beauty and connection. And through it all, I continue to chart a new path, one that honors my true self and empowers others to do the same.

Working on what's next

My experiences led me to create two spaces for people to come to share their unique experiences and work on healing. Creating The Life Lab and Half Moon Mental Health and Wellness were milestones on this journey, marking the transition from understanding to action. These ventures allowed me to put into practice a holistic approach to healing, one that recognizes the individuality of each person's journey and offers a space for comprehensive care. By incorporating strategies that range from traditional therapy to mindfulness, coaching, and movement, I aim to provide a pathway to wellness that is as individual as each person I work with.

The Life Lab offers a nurturing space that addresses personal, professional, and emotional development through Mindset Coaching. The goal is to help individuals set and achieve their goals in a way that makes sense to them.

Half Moon Mental Health and Wellness operates from the belief that effective mental health care must account for all aspects of a person's health. Every person that comes through the door gets a personalized approach that is as unique as they are. Various therapeutic and wellness strategies are used to ensure every person has the support and tools they need to thrive in all aspects of their lives.

My personal stories, from the struggles of my youth to the triumphs and setbacks of adulthood, have been integral to this mission. They have not only shaped my understanding of resilience and recovery but have also allowed me to connect with my clients on a deeply empathetic level. I share my journey openly, not as a tale of hardship, but as a testament to the possibility of transformation and to show you that you are not alone. Through my work, I aim to inspire those I work with to embrace their whole selves, acknowledging their pain while also recognizing their inherent strength and capacity for healing.

As I reflect on the path that led me to where I am today, I am filled with gratitude for the lessons learned and the challenges overcome. My quest for belonging and understanding has evolved into a lifelong mission to empower others, guiding them toward well-being that nurtures mind, body, and spirit. This is not just my story; it's a call to action for anyone seeking to reclaim their health and happiness through a more integrated, compassionate approach to healing.

I invite you to join me in this movement toward well-being. Reflect on your story, recognize the strength in your struggles, and take steps toward a healthier, more integrated life. Whether it's seeking support, starting a dialogue about mental health, or simply embracing your journey, every step forward is a step toward healing not just yourself, but our community as a whole.

Let's take this journey together, from struggle to strength, and transform our challenges into our greatest assets.

Visit alexisenterline.com or
halfmoonmentalhealthandwellness.com
for more information.

If you are ready to be visible from the inside out, be showcased on podcasts, be asked to present in front of new and exciting audiences, work on your own story, become a published author, and help hundreds of women on their way to their own greatness while experiencing a life-transforming journey of writing a book, Join the **Ati.G.Branding Ascension Mastermind**.

A one-of-a-kind experience to build your personal brand, bring your message to the world, and forever have your story imprinted in the world.

Bringing who you are into what you do at a whole new level. For more information, registration, or to join the waitlist, visit: www.atigrinspun.com/ascensionmastermind